Howard Hughes:
THE LAS VEGAS YEARS

The Women, the Mormons, the Mafia

JOHN HARRIS SHERIDAN

authorHOUSE®

AuthorHouse™
1663 Liberty Drive
Bloomington, IN 47403
www.authorhouse.com
Phone: 1-800-839-8640

johnharrissheridan.com

First published by AuthorHouse 8/31/2011

ISBN: 978-1-4634-0695-0 (sc)
ISBN: 978-1-4634-0694-3 (hc)
ISBN: 978-1-4634-0693-6 (e)

Library of Congress Control Number: 2011908553

Printed in the United States of America

Dedicated to:

Thomas J. Sheridan, brother
John Patrick Sheridan, son
Kevin Kelly Sheridan, son
Thomas Brendan Sheridan, son

Acknowledgements

Gary Sotir: A talented and sensitive television executive, and a true and honest friend, without whose many contributions this book would never have made it out of the typewriter.

Nacho Garcia: An award winning artist from The El Paso Times newspaper. His renderings of people who have passed into history have brought them back to life. I'm honored to have worked with Nacho Garcia.

Bill Seffel: Las Vegas, Nevada; for his countless hours of driving to Tonopah, Goldfield, and Lida Nevada taking pictures of the Cottontail Ranch, the air strip, and securing copies of the Hughes marriage certificate. Bill grew up in Las Vegas and was a card dealer in one of the mob owned hotels. He spent the majority of his life around the people in this book. I'm very grateful to Bill Seffel.

Oralia Ortega: Television anchor, who never let me think of anything else but the book. I'm almost grateful!

Sergio Rodriguez, El Paso, Texas: For his much needed help and computer expertise, redoing the manuscript time and time again.

Ryan Hall: Las Cruces, New Mexico: For his photographic talent on the back of this book "About the Author" taking an old subject and making it look presentable.

Bianca Olivas, El Paso, Texas: For her wonderful artwork.

Contents

Arriving in
LAS VEGAS

IT WAS A COLD NOVEMBER NIGHT night in Nevada in 1966, a train was stopped a couple of miles outside of the city of Las Vegas. Why the train stopped there, very few people knew. However, three black limousines and a Ford Econoline van were waiting right next to the train. The door of the private Pullman car opened, and six men carried out a stretcher that appeared to have a person on it. The person was wrapped from head to toe in blankets and was carried to the Ford van. At one time in the 1930s, that person had received a ticker tape parade down Broadway. He set flying records around the world, comparable to Charles Lindberg's.

Two men dressed in expensive suits got out of one of the limousines and started giving orders. One man was a former member of the FBI and CIA. The other was one of the biggest mobsters in the country. He represented the Fratellanza, also known as the Mafia or the Chicago Syndicate. He represented Los Angeles and Las Vegas, as well as the five New York families that ran the Mafia. It was a rather strange combination of men.

The man on the stretcher was a reclusive billionaire, who owned one of the biggest airlines in the world, TWA Air Lines, and a major motion picture studio, RKO Pictures. He slept with some of the most glamorous actresses in the world. He was a big part of Hollywood's Golden Era, an enigmatic movie producer and director who was seen in the best night clubs in Los Angeles. The man now wrapped in blankets had at one time walked into the Copacabana, Ciro's, and the Coconut Grove in Hollywood dressed in an expensive black tuxedo and white sneakers, with Katharine Hepburn or Ava Gardner on his arm. Of course, Ava was the source of his legendary feud with Frank Sinatra. However, many people believed that he and Jane Russell were lovers since their first movie, *The Outlaw.* But according to Jane and her brother Jamie, Howard and Jane remained friends for more than thirty-five years, and their relationship never went any further than that.

The man they called the "Wiseguy" ran Las Vegas. He owned that town. Known for his good looks and expensive Italian suits, he was allegedly involved in the assassination of a president and a movie star and the attempted assassination of a dictator. That didn't stop "Handsome Johnny" from working with the CIA or the man on the stretcher; it just didn't matter. His friends said he never lied, except to cops and judges. Anywhere else in the United States this would have been breaking news, but in Las Vegas, it was an everyday event. Nobody cared; nobody batted an eye—nobody even dared.

The former federal agent was known as "Mr. Fix-it.." He got things done for the man on the stretcher, and that's why he was paid a fortune. He went from Washington, DC to Las Vegas, to the top of the world, making $10,000.00 a week (in 1966 dollars), with an endless expense account. But he never saw the man on the stretcher face to face, the man who paid him more than half a million dollars a year—the man who gave him two Cadillac cars, a mansion on the Desert Inn Golf Course that the locals called "Little Caesar's Palace," and a large yacht in Newport Beach, California.

By now I'm sure you guessed it. The man on the stretcher was none other than the reclusive billionaire and aviator Howard Robard Hughes Jr. He had always loved Las Vegas, and this time he intended to stay for good. He spent a lot of time there in the 40s and 50s. He brought his girlfriends there, many of whom were movie stars or contract players. He gambled in Las Vegas, purchased property, and bought homes he never lived in. This time, it was all going to be different. This time, he had plans for Las Vegas, to the point of moving Hughes Aircraft there; he even bought property to do just that.

Hughes intended to live in Las Vegas forever. He planned to build the world's largest "super hotel" by adding four thousand rooms to the Sands, one of his hotels, and putting in a shopping center and a motion picture theater, as well as an ice skating rink and an indoor eighteen-hole golf course, a bowling ally, and an indoor motor bike track. The amazing thing is that motor bikes weren't even popular yet. He told his aides that the hotel would be a city in itself. Hughes had many, many plans, but few materialized.

The limousine convoy led by the three black limousines took off down Sahara Boulevard toward Las Vegas Boulevard South and turned right on the Strip toward the Desert Inn Hotel and Country Club. The limousines were Hughes's idea, to create confusion at the time of his arrival. Hughes hated crowds, cameras, and on-lookers. Just as he had planned, the limousines pulled up to the front doors of the Desert Inn, creating quite a spectacle. Everyone, including some of the employees, assumed a group of movie stars or other celebrities had arrived. The hotel guests stood around for autographs, waiting for someone to exit the limousines. While they were waiting, the van drove to the employee entrance, and Hughes entered the hotel from the driveway on Desert Inn Road, north of the hotel. By the time the crowd outside realized that nobody was going to get out of the three limousines, Hughes was tucked away on his Barcalounger in the ninth floor penthouse. This was the beginning of the biggest thing to ever happen to Las Vegas …

Desert Inn Hotel: circa 1966

Desert Inn Hotel: circa 1966

THE DESERT

The Rumble in

HUGHES WAS EXUBERANT. HE WAS in love with Las Vegas and glad to be out of the big cities. The only problem was his wife, movie actress Jean Peters. Jean hated the desert, and she hated hotels even more. All she ever wanted was a home—not much to ask from a billionaire. She really didn't care where it was, just so it wasn't in the desert, but it wasn't to be. Hughes offered her a home he already owned, though he never stepped foot in it. It was in Las Vegas and, you guessed it, it was in the desert, like everything else in Las Vegas. It included 517 acres of land (sand). The place was known as the Krupp Ranch, and it was located in Green Valley. Hughes purchased it from Vera Krupp, sight unseen, for $980,000.00. Vera was a German actress who had been married to Alfried Krupp, owner of the notorious German Krupp Defense Works, which became famous during World War II working for Hitler and the Nazi government.

Vera moved to Las Vegas. She made some very bad investments

with the wrong people and lost a lot of money, under rather unusual circumstances. She got involved with some people from Chicago and lost millions of dollars ….Capice?

Before Howard Hughes moved to Nevada, he told Moe Dalitz, the Desert Inn owner, he only intended to stay ten days or so; however, he and the "Mormon Mafia" were starting day twenty, and it was beginning to annoy the owner of the hotel. You didn't want to annoy Moe Dalitz, no matter who you were. It was annoying to Moe, because Hughes occupied the eighth and ninth floors; the hotel needed the rooms for their high rollers during the busy New Year's season. Hughes was paying $28,000 a day for the two floors he and his people occupied, but that amount was nothing! Moe was beginning to realize that having "Big Howard" taking up so much room was costing him big bucks, because Moe had nowhere to put his 'high rollers, and it was possible they might go to another hotel. On top of that, Hughes's Mormons made no contribution to the hotel at all. They didn't drink, they didn't smoke, and, worst of all, they didn't gamble. That was enough to make a saint swear—a Latter Day Saint!

Organized crime still owned most of the big Strip hotels in the 60s and 70s, and the Desert Inn Hotel and Country Club was no exception. The public was told on television, radio, and in the newspapers that the Desert Inn Hotel and Country Club was owned by Wilber Clark. It was always referred to as "Wilber Clark's Desert Inn Hotel and Country Club." That's what they told ya, that's what they wanted ya to believe. In reality the owner was Morris Barney "Moe" Dalitz and his group. Who was Morris Barney "Moe" Dalitz? In his latter years he was one of the most beloved hotel/casino owners in Las Vegas. Moe was a citizen any city would be glad to claim. He was instrumental in the construction of Sunrise Hospital, the biggest private hospital west of Chicago at that time. He built the Boulevard Mall, Las Vegas's first major shopping mall; The Las Vegas Country Club was followed by the Sunrise Hospital and The Rancho La Costa, in Southern California.

Dalitz even received awards from the states of Nevada and California and Israel. But Moe didn't get to the top by being "Mr. Nice Guy." The hospital that Moe built had two functions. One was humanitarian, caring for the sick. The other was a more fiduciary consideration, and that was to move the skim money, considered a tribute, to the Mafia families back East. Imagine building a hospital to move skim money out of town; but that's what Moe did. The Nevada Gaming Commission, and the Las Vegas Metropolitan Police Department, as well as the FBI, were starting to catch on to the skim game. They knew millions of non-taxable dollars were leaving Las Vegas each day; they knew most of the hotels were doing it, but they just couldn't figure out how. Moe figured out how. He built a hospital.

I know you're wondering how a hospital could help the casino owners illegally move skim money out of Las Vegas to Kansas City and Chicago. Here is how Moe did it. Moe would have a pseudo patient fly into Las Vegas on a private plane and be taken to Sunrise Hospital by ambulance. After a couple of days the patient would returned to the plane, this time with the skim money on the gurney.

All the law enforcement agencies knew was a patient arrived at Sunrise Hospital and returned home shortly thereafter; but they never figured out the real mission. And the Mafia got richer and richer. It was about this time the FBI put the Las Vegas Police Department on its "Don't Share Information" List because they learned that certain members of the police department were sharing information with organized crime members. That lasted a little over a year.

Moe Dalitz was once a member of the notorious Purple Gang in Detroit. The Purple Gang was made up of primarily Jewish mobsters who were extremely ruthless in their dealings. When the FBI started to move in on the Purple Gang, Moe moved out; later he moved to Ohio and became associated with Al Polizzi and the Cleveland Mafia. His willingness to use strong-arm tactics earned him the admiration and respect of Charles "Lucky" Luciano, Frank Costello, and Meyer Lansky. It was about this time that Meyer Lansky and his people took over the Flamingo Hotel, after Bugsy Siegel was murdered in Beverly Hills at his girlfriend Virginia Hill's home. Bugsy misappropriated some six million dollars of Mafia money and refused to return it. It's been said his best friend Meyer Lansky ordered the hit. Others say it wasn't a Mafia hit at all, that Virginia Hill's brother made the hit, tired of Bugsy beating up his sister.

Meyer Lansky had the Flamingo running like a Swiss watch in less than a year's time and making big money. Lansky had an interest in the Thunderbird Hotel, as well as the Sands Hotel and Country Club and the El Cortez Hotel in downtown Las Vegas with Frank Costello. Lansky and Costello brought Frank Sinatra to the Sands, where he stayed. Later he join up with the Rat Pack and filled the place with tourists and gangsters, until Maheu had him removed in the mid-sixties, on the orders of Hughes. (More on that later.) The New England Mafia, aka the Patriarca family, was even involved in Las Vegas, running the Dunes Hotel. Sinatra's pal Sam Giancana from Chicago and the Fischetti brothers had a big interest in the Sahara and Riviera. The Mafia ran Las Vegas, and most of the time it did a better job than the corporations that run the hotel/casinos today. Almost all of the lounge shows were free, featuring well-known entertainers, like the Kim Sisters, Johnny Ray, Waylon Jennings, Brendan Bowyer, the DeJohn Sisters, Jerry Vale, and even Wayne

Newton, many of whom graduated to the main show room, such as "Mr. Las Vegas," Wayne Newton.

Before he came to Las Vegas, Dalitz was involved in illegal gambling in West Virginia, Kentucky, and Indiana. He became one of the two most powerful Jewish gangsters in the United States, along with Meyer Lansky, Bugsy Siegal's ex-partner. Moe Dalitz, Meyer Lansky, and Bugsy Siegal weren't actual "made" members of the Mafia because, a made member had to be Italian or Sicilian, and on orders from the Mafia they had to have killed someone. Being Jewish, they didn't qualify for regular membership. So they became associate members, and as such, with their influence, knowledge, and loyalty to the organization and its bosses, they had even more power and clout than a Mafia *capo* (boss). Charles "Lucky" Luciano always thought the world of Meyer Lansky and Moe Dalitz and didn't care whether they were Italian or not; over the objection of other members, he made sure they were always included when he was choosing those to attend meetings of the La Cosa Nostra (Mafia). And whatever Luciano said was *law* … Mafia law.

Luciano was the Godfather, or *Copo di tutti Capi*, the Boss of all Bosses, Chairman of the Commission. The Commission is the organization that runs the five major Mafia families: The Bonanno family, the Gambino family, the Colombo family, the Lucchese family, and the Genovese family, as well as the twenty-six lesser families within the United States …

Mafia Ranks & Terms

Copo di Tutti Capi = Boss of all Bosses, Godfather or Don
Under Boss = Second in Command in a Mafia Family
Consigliore = The advisor to the Godfather, not always a
      lawyer

Caporegime = Upper management in a Mafia Family
Capo = A middle-management Mafioso
Copodecina = A supervisor who manages ten soldiers
Fratellanza = Italian for brotherhood, another name for
              Mafia
A Friend of Ours = A Mafioso, a member of the crime
              family
A Friend of Mine = A trusted friend, a connected person.
              Not a member of the Mafia.
Comare = A Mafia girlfriend, a term of endearment

It wasn't good or even healthy to have Moe mad at you. Finally, Moe couldn't take Howard's antics any longer. Now the fight begins: Moe "The Destroyer" Dalitz vs. Howard "The Aviator" Hughes. This fight could be bigger than the Rumble in the Jungle between Mohammed Ali and George Foreman. It could have been billed as the Disaster in the Desert:

Round 1 = Moe tells Maheu to tell Hughes to get his ass out of the hotel ASAP or he was going to have him thrown out.

Round 2 = Maheu relayed the massage to Hughes, and Hughes said, "Bob, I like it here. Tell Dalitz I'm not moving." This response sent chills down Maheu's back. Hughes was a billionaire all right; but Dalitz could have a man killed with a phone call.

Round 3 = Johnny Roselli becomes involved. Why is a high-ranking Mafia capo coming to the aide of Hughes? Bob Maheu doesn't know what to do. He talked with Moe and Moe's partner Ruby Kolod, and they both wanted Hughes out before Christmas. So Maheu called Johnny Roselli, who can fix anything, except his car.

Round 4 = Roselli calls Jimmy Hoffa in Detroit. At that time, Hoffa was president of the powerful International Brotherhood of Teamsters and, as such, he was very influential in the Teamsters Central States Pension Fund, the organization that floated loans to all Mafia-owned hotels. Roselli explains the problem to Jimmy Hoffa and asks for his help. So Hoffa calls Moe. ... Roselli calls Moe. ... and Moe, who is intimidated by no man, finally relents over his friendship with Roselli and Hoffa and allows Hughes to stay a little while longer. Johnny Roselli is also living at the Desert Inn, as well as keeping an apartment at the Diplomat on Paradise Road, less than a mile away. The last thing he needs is trouble in Paradise. Johnny also has an office in the Desert Inn, called the Monte Presser Talent Agency. This agency never used Johnny's name, however. It booked almost all of the major acts on the Strip, and it was the most successful agency in Las Vegas. The Monte Presser Agency handled the big production shows, as well as major stars appearing on the Strip, making millions of dollars, much of the money going to Chicago ... Capice?

Round 5 = Johnny Roselli calls Maheu and tells him he should tell Hughes to buy the Desert Inn, and his problems would be solved. Roselli tells Maheu to tell Hughes to offer Moe more than the place is worth, and he'll get the deal. Maheu agrees and proposes the idea to Hughes, pointing out the tax advantages to Hughes of passive versus active income, saying that buying the hotel would bring enormous tax advantages. On top of that, Nevada has no state income tax. That's all Hughes needed to hear. He hated paying taxes of any kind. So he tells Maheu to make the deal with Dalitz.

Round 6 = Hughes offers Dalitz $13.25 million, and Moe accepts. The hotel was thought to be worth between six and seven million. So the fight turned out to be a draw. Hughes got the hotel he wanted for almost twice its value, and Moe and the Mob got the money. In Las Vegas, it wasn't so much what you know, as much as who you know.

Meyer Lansky born Majer Suchowlinski in Grodno, Russia.
He was the brains behind the mob (7/4/1902–1/15/1983).

Morris Barney 'Moe' Dalitz, born in Boston, MA. ...
bootlegger, racketeer, Casino owner. He shaped Las Vegas
into the modern city it is today (12/25/1899–1/15/1983).

Johnny Roselli, born Filippo Socco. the Mob's man in Los Angeles and Las Vegas. Had ties with the CIA (7/4/1905–8/9/1976).

Robert Maheu, Chief Executive Officer: Hughes Nevada Operations.

The Showman
& MOE

IN 1969 I GOT TO know Moe Dalitz through a friend of mine named Bob Williams, one of American's great entertainers living in Las Vegas. Bob Williams lived next door to Moe on Desert Inn Road, on the Desert Inn Golf Course. Bob started out in vaudeville and later had one of the greatest dog acts in show business, called "Bob Williams and his Dog Louie." It took a lot of training to get Louie to do what he did in the act, and that was absolutely nothing. That's what was so funny. Bob did the work, and Louie did nothing. Bob appeared many times on *The Ed Sullivan Show*, *The Steve Allen Show*, and *The Colgate Comedy Hour*. Bob had a long run at the Tropicana Hotel in Las Vegas, in the Folies Bergere. He was a regular on the 70s TV show called *Fernwood Tonight*, produced by Norman Lear in 1977. Bob played the security guard. .

Bob purchased a lot of property in Nevada and Malibu, in Southern California. He had a horse ranch in Malibu and a beautiful home in Las Vegas. Bob was a very smart investor, and he made a lot of money. Subsequently he purchased a home next to Moe Dalitz in Las Vegas, and that's how I met Moe.

I would visit Bob Williams at his home a couple of times a week, and many times Moe would be there too. Bob and Moe were friends for years. And because of Bob, I got to know Moe pretty well. Bob would tell Moe things about my early life, such as after graduating from high school, I joined Ice Capades as an ice skater for a few years; for some reason Moe was very interested in the whole Ice Capades thing. He used to tease me about skating around in, as he called it, "Those tight sequined pants." To set the record straight, I never wore sequined pants. I think the fact that John Harris, my mother's brother and my uncle, started the show in 1940, and his wife, Donna Atwood, was the star of the show for years intrigued him. Believe it or not, he knew exactly who they were, and he even remembered seeing Donna in at the Pan Pacific Auditorium in Los Angeles. But what intrigued me more was the fact that Moe knew all about the show and my uncle, John Harris. He was able to name the old skating stars of the past, and that just amazed me. I really think he had a crush on Sonja Henie as a young man. He knew all of her movies and always said how beautiful she was. And as I later learned in the 50s, Moe even hired a former Ice Capades choreographer to do shows for him on the Strip. His name was Donn Arden, and he became a very famous choreographer and show director in Las Vegas and Reno and in motion pictures. Donn set the standard for the Las Vegas showgirl when he debuted "Lido de Paris" at the Stardust Hotel and became known as "the Father of Feathers."

It's funny now; but when Moe wasn't looking at me, I would be looking at him and, thinking, *He's just like a granddad or an old uncle.* Many times I wondered, *Did he really order the Purple Gang or the*

Mafia to kill people? I've been told he did, and I read that he did, but I never wanted to believe it. I still find it very difficult to believe what the cops and others have told me. I know Moe knew things about Hughes, but he never said a bad word about him or, for that matter, a good word about him either. I don't think he liked the Hughes aides much, except maybe for John Holmes, and I don't know why.

Moe Dalitz in his later years.

Meyer Lansky in his later years.

The Huge Hughes
SHOPPING SPREE

HUGHES LOVED OWNING THE DESERT Inn Hotel and felt more a part of the community because of it. He especially loved the tax advantages. About 3 am one morning, he called Bob Maheu and woke him out of a sound sleep. Hughes was used to watching television at that hour, but television signed off the air about 12:30 am in Las Vegas, and he had nothing to do. Remember, there were no VHS recorders, DVDs, or cable in those days. So, Hughes had his Mormons (that's what he called them) call the stations and request more movies, but the stations wouldn't oblige him. Hughes thought about buying a television station but put it off at that time. He finally got Bob on the phone and said, "Bob, I want you to look around and see how many of these hotels and casinos are for sale. Let's buy as many as we can." Bob agreed, hung up the phone, and went back to sleep. He had a meeting with the governor in the morning, because Hughes refused to appear before the gaming commission, and they were trying to work around that requirement. Governor Paul Laxalt felt he could get the State Gaming Commission to go along with Hughes on this request, because as the governor said, "Having Hughes involved in the gaming industry is like having the Good Housekeeping Seal of Approval." And he was right. Hughes brought respectability to a city overrun by organized crime. That's what everyone thought anyway.

Paul Laxalt for PRESIDENT

GOVERNOR LAXALT WAS ALWAYS TRYING to improve the gaming image in Nevada. Paul Laxalt may have been the best governor Nevada ever had. He kept taxes low, brought new industries to Nevada, and promoted the state as a place where a family could have good, clean fun at a bargain price. He knew that bringing Hughes to Nevada at a time when the economy was hurting was going to be good for the state. In no time at all, the Nevada Gaming Commission approved Hughes's application. Then Hughes was ready to do some serious shopping. Due to a settlement with TWA, he had a little over a half a billion dollars to spend, and in 1968 that made him the richest man in the United States. Howard Hughes was also America's first billionaire; J. Paul Getty was second. Hughes went on the biggest shopping spree Nevada had ever seen. He bought the Desert Inn for $13.25 million, the Sands for $14.6 million; the Castaways for $3 million; the Frontier for $14 million; the Silver Slipper for $5.3

million; the Landmark, for $17.3 million, and Harold's Club, in Reno, for $10.5 million.

During my years in Nevada I got to know Senator Paul Laxalt through his sister, a Catholic nun named Sister Sue. Sister Sue ran the Catholic Community Services Center in Reno and later in Las Vegas. Sister Sue did more good for the Church than anybody I know. She was definitely the Mother Theresa of Nevada, and her brother, the senator, left Nevada better than he found it. The Laxalts were a special gift to Nevada. Paul Laxalt left the US Senate and went into the practice of law in Washington, DC.

Few people know it, but Senator Paul Laxalt was President Ronald Reagan's first choice for vice president of the United States, but Senator Laxalt refused the offer because the *Sacramento Bee* newspaper claimed a hotel in Carson City in which Senator Laxalt owned stock received loans from the Teamsters Central States Pension Fund, overseen by Jimmy Hoffa. It was the organization that funded Mafia hotels. So Senator Laxalt thought that would bring bad press to the Reagan campaign, and he recommended George H. W. Bush for the job. Later, the *Sacramento Bee* dropped its assertions. That action on the part of the *Sacramento Bee* deprived the USA of a great vice president, and possibly a president.

NACHO GARCIA

*Paul Laxalt, born Reno, Nevada 8/2/1922; Nevada U.S.
senator and governor. Hughes's pick for President.*

Somewhere Over
THE RAINBOW
at the Riviera

P HIL RICHARDS, ONE OF THE producers of my brother and sister's show at the Aladdin, was also a makeup artist for Judy Garland. One night he asked me if I wanted to go over to the Rivera Hotel to see Judy's show and meet her. Well, that was a no-brainer, so I accompanied Phil to the Rivera to see Judy Garland. I remember the hotel was really crowded that night; I just assumed it was because of Judy. When we arrived backstage and went into Judy's dressing room, I couldn't believe what I saw. Two people were feeding her mashed potatoes and black coffee. She was so intoxicated she could hardly talk. When Phil introduced her to me, she shook my hand and mumbled something. I had no idea what she said.

She was very thin. I don't see how she could have weighed more than eighty-five or ninety pounds. She was four feet ten inches, maybe five feet tall at the most. I could hardly believe it. What's more, I couldn't imagine her going on stage in that condition. Suddenly a stage hand arrived and took me up to the light booth to watch the show. The show started about ten minutes late. The music was "Somewhere Over the Rainbow," and the announcer said, Ladies and gentlemen, the Rivera Hotel proudly presents … Miss Judy Garland!" I felt so sorry for her; in her condition, I thought it was going to be a disaster, but I couldn't believe what came next. Judy walked out on stage as confident and composed as Kristi Yamaguchi in *Dancing with the Stars*. I couldn't believe my eyes. You couldn't tell she ever had a drink, and she gave one of the greatest performances I had ever seen. After the show I mentioned my surprise over Judy's performance to Phil. I said she acted like she never had a drink, and he said, "I don't know how she does it either; but she does it every night."

Judy Garland. Picked as one of the ten greatest female American movie stars. Died in London of a drug overdose. (6/10/1922–6/22/1969)

Hughes Tries to Buy
THE STARDUST

BACK IN LAS VEGAS, HOWARD Hughes tried his best to buy the Stardust, for $32 million, but the federal government stepped in and said Hughes would have a monopoly and stopped the sale. So instead of the Stardust going to Hughes, the Stardust ended up with the Argent Corporation, headed by Alan R. Glick, an unwilling front for the Mafia. In fact, the Stardust Hotel became so infected with underworld activity that it became the subject of a major motion picture.

The picture was called *Casino*. In reality, it was the story of the Stardust Hotel, but in the movie it was called, the Tangiers. *Casino*, written by Nicholas Pileggi and directed by Martin Scorsese, was the most accurate depiction of crime in a hotel or casino in Las Vegas ever reported. Robert DeNiro played Sam "Ace" Rothstein, who in real life was Frank "Lefty" Rosenthal. Frank couldn't get licensed by the Nevada Gaming Commission as a key employee because of a series of arrests for fixing college basketball games, So he was everything from vice president and general manager, to assistant PR manager, to food and beverage manager, to entertainment director, to the host of his own television show, *The Frank Rosenthal Show* seen on KSHO-TV, Channel 13, the ABC affiliate in Las Vegas.

Having his own television show really bothered the Mafia members back in Chicago and Kansas City, because it was anything but low profile and unassuming, and the Mafia liked low profile and unassuming. At the hotels at that time, if you were unable to become a key employee because of prior convictions or even associations, you just changed your job title to one that didn't require a key employee endorsement from the Gaming Commission, like a job that wasn't directly involved with gaming. You were cleared to work that job until the Gaming Commission caught up with you again, which could take years. Some people worked for more than fifteen years without becoming key employees.

Everyone knew Lefty was running the casino, even the cops, and that's the way it was in Las Vegas. Besides being connected, Lefty was one of the greatest odds makers ever to set foot in a casino or sports book—any casino or sports book, anywhere. He was just friends with the wrong guys and broke a law or two. He was pals with Joey Auippa, Frank Balistrieri, Nick Civella, Carl DeLuna, Anthony John Spilotro, and more. In the movie *Casino*, Joe Pesci played Nicky Santoro, who in real life was Anthony J. Spilotro, better known in Las Vegas as Tony "The Ant" Spilotro, or "The Little Guy," because he was only about five foot three.

But then, a pit bull is a little guy too. Tony was about as tough as you get; he was literally a killer. If you beat him with a bat, he'd come back with a knife. If you beat him with a knife, he'd come back with a gun, and he'd keep coming back until one of you was dead, and chances are it would be you. The Las Vegas Metropolitan Police Department told me he's responsible for twenty-seven to thirty murders. So who did the Chicago mob send to Las Vegas to protect their interests? Tony Spilotro. They sent Spilotro to watch after all of their interests, as well as to protect their money-maker, Frank "Lefty" Rosenthal, because he was making so much cash for the mob, they never wanted anything to happen to him.

Lefty ran the Stardust like a drill sergeant runs basic training, and Tony took care of the more unpleasant activities, like trouble makers, cheats, slow-payers, even dishonest employees. However, their friendship came to an end when Tony started cheating on his wife with Lefty's wife. In the movie *Casino,* Lefty's wife was played by the beautiful Sharon Stone, who was nominated for an Oscar for playing the part of Ginger McKenna Rothstein (real name Gerri McGee Rosenthal). Gerri was an exquisitely beautiful topless showgirl in the Folies Bergere at the Tropicana Hotel who supplemented her income by chip hustling and hooking on the side. Lefty knew about it before he married her; but she was so beautiful, I guess it didn't matter to him.

As time went on, Spilotro was getting way out of line. He had been placed in Nevada Gaming's Black Book, which meant he couldn't go into a casino, not even for a pack of cigarettes. He was bringing a lot of unwanted publicity to Lefty Rosenthal, the Stardust, and most importantly organized crime in general. The mob in Chicago got wind of Tony's antics in Las Vegas. The fact was that he was also under criminal indictment, as well as being involved in high profile crimes with his "Hole in the Wall Gang," a group of mobsters who broke into the homes of wealthy local people, taking hundreds of thousands of dollars in cash, without sending The Outfit its percentage—a very bad thing to do.

Many homes in the Sun Belt areas, like Phoenix, Tucson, Albuquerque, El Paso, and Las Vegas, are built with stucco walls. They're great in the winter for keeping heat in and in the summer for keeping the home cool. However, gaining entry to a stucco home is not particularly difficult. And since most people in Las Vegas guard their privacy with walls around their homes, it's just that much easier to break in—who is going to see you? So Tony's gang became known by the Las Vegas Metropolitan Police and the local media as The Hole in the Wall Gang, so named because of their method of gaining entry into a home with a sledge hammer. Tony Spilotro and his guys could gain entry in approximately three minutes. They would pound out a hole in the wall, use wire cutters to cut away the chicken wire, punch a hole through the dry wall, and they were, in the home in three minutes or less. However, the Mafia bosses back in Chicago kept hearing about Spilotro's freelance escapades. They weren't getting their cut, which was mandatory, and they were pissed off.

Casino customers were also a big target of Tony Spilotro and his boyhood pal Frank Cullotta. He had the help of hotel employees, who were on his payroll—just supplementing their income a little bit, that's all. They included staff like the front desk clerks, bellhops, bartenders, valet parking attendants, maids, and even cab drivers. These people would call Tony, Frank Cullotta, or Michael Spilotro, Tony's brother, and tell them there was a big spender in a certain room and whether they were in or not, at the present time. Then Spilotro's gang would go to work and clean out all the valuables from the hotel room.

Spiloto was also running the town's biggest shylock operation and, as usual, never kicked back a percentage of his take to the mob in Chicago. Before Spilotro took over the shylock business, it was run by a guy named Jasper Especial. Jasper was actually a very nice guy. My friends and I used to have Italian food quite often in his restaurant. You would never suspect him for a Mafioso; but all the locals in town knew he was, and the Metropolitan Police Department knew it as well. Jasper was owner of The Leaning Tower of Pizza on the Strip, past the Dunes, and he served the best pizza in town. Jasper always paid a percentage of his take to Chicago, so they knew approximately what they should be getting from Spilotro, and they were getting nothing.

Another thing—Jasper was a good shylock. If you couldn't pay him right away, he always gave you time. But it wasn't that way with Tony. The first time you had no money—no teeth. The second time no money—no life. And you would be found floating in Lake Meade, which was another no-no, because he wasn't suppose to make a mob killing in Las Vegas. And on top of all of that, he was having an affair with an associate's wife, Gerri McGee Rosenthal. Gerri was Lefty's wife, which was strictly against the Mafia code. You never mess around with another member's wife or girlfriend. As it turned out, a couple of years before, Gerri had an affair with Tony Spilotro out of town. They met in Chicago, at a gaming convention she attended to promote The Tropicana's Folies Bergere stage show, in which she was a topless dancer. Gerri and Tony met in a bar at the Conrad Hilton Hotel. That all took place before she knew her soon-to-be husband, Frank "Lefty" Rosenthal. So I guess Gerri and Tony just couldn't leave each other alone, and the tryst continued.

The old Mafia bosses back in Chicago and Kansas City couldn't put up with that kind of behavior. So once The Outfit got word about it, Spilotro had signed his own death certificate. And getting word of Spilotro's affairs to the Mafia bosses back in Chicago was pretty easy, because it was in the *Las Vegas Sun* and the *Review Journal* newspapers nearly every day. And news was put there by the Las Vegas Metropolitan Police Department (LVMPD) and the FBI exactly to alert the bosses back home and let them know what their little "Ant" was up to in Las Vegas. The cops knew this was tantamount to putting out a contract on Spilotro. What was never mentioned in the papers was Spilotro's affair with a little Mormon girl who he met in the hospital. Her name was Sheryl, and she looked about sixteen, even though she said she was in her twenties. Spilotro really fell hard for this young girl. He bought her a new car, a Plymouth Fury, and a seventy five thousand dollar two-bedroom condo near Flamingo and Eastern. The problem with that was it angered many of the high-powered City Council members and County Commission members, who were mostly Mormons, as well as the sheriff, who was also a Mormon. Just another reason to get Spilotro out of town, forever.

Michael Spilotro was Tony's brother and partner in their jewelry store, The Gold Rush, on West Sahara. That was one of the places they fenced some of the stolen jewelry, among other things. The brothers went to Chicago for what they thought was a celebration over beating a federal indictment; instead, the brothers were beaten with baseball bats, tortured and buried alive in their underwear, a Mafia insult. They were found by mistake on an Indiana farm owned by Chicago mob boss Joey Auippa, who took over after the murder of mob boss Sam Giancana. Imagine Auippa's surprise when he learned what happened to the two Spilotro brothers who were found on his property. Joey had only recently learned about it, when he read it in the newspaper. If you believe that, you'll believe Al Gore invented the Internet.

Frank "Lefty" Rosenthal, the gangster played by Robert DeNiro in the movie Casino. He was the greatest odds-maker in the business (6/12/1929–10/13/2008).

Gerri McGee Rosenthal, married to Frank "Lefty" Rosenthal.
She was a former dancer at the Folies Bergere, a chip hustler,
and a part-time hooker (5/16/1936–11/9/1982).

NACHO GARCIA

Tony "The Ant" Spilotro was the mob enforcer for the Chicago Outfit. He was played by Joe Pesci in the movie Casino (5/19/1938–6/14/1986)

Joey Auippa, boss of the Chicago Outfit, after Sam Giancana.

It Could Have Been His
FINAL DRINK

ONE EVENING AROUND 8 PM, about a mile from the Stardust Hotel, Frank "Lefty" Rosenthal was having a sandwich and a couple of drinks at Tony Roma's on East Sahara. Lefty was with a couple of his friends from the Stardust, as he was every week at that time. You could set your watch by his arrival time, and, apparently, the would-be murderers did just that.

When Lefty got into his car to start back home to tuck his young children into bed, his car blew up, almost killing him. The bombers didn't know it, but that model Cadillac had a metal plate under the driver's seat, which saved Lefty's life. Lefty rolled out of the car onto the cement driveway, and a second explosion tossed the car twenty feet in the air. Two civilians and an Alcohol, Tobacco and Firearms (ATF) agent who happened to be in the area shielded Lefty from the falling debris. Lieutenant Danny Mahony was among the first Las Vegas Metropolitan Police officers on the scene and couldn't believe

Lefty survived. Mahony said, "His face, his left arm, and the hair on the left side of his head were burned, I can't imagine he survived this." The question still remains—who did it? The Las Vegas Metropolitan Police Department believe it was arranged by Tony Spolitro and executed by two killers from Chicago who the LVMPD later arrested; however, they were let go due to lack of evidence. The FBI under Joe Yablonsky, special agent in charge of the Las Vegas office, believes it was carried out on the orders of Frank Balistieri, the Mafia boss of Milwaukee, who was known as "The Mad Bomber" while he worked his way up to Mafia boss. However, the two men who were held in custody by the Las Vegas Metropolitan Police could have been sent to Las Vegas by either Tony Spilotro or Frank Balistieri. The Mafia was beginning to think Lefty was getting a little too much notoriety: because of his TV show, which they hated; his wife Gerri's affair with "The Ant"; his immense ego; and his lawsuits against the state of Nevada and the Nevada Gaming Commission. All of which gave the Mafia unwanted publicity. So they didn't lift a finger to stop the action against Lefty. Frank Balistieri was the guy who put Allen Glick together with the Teamsters Central States Pension Fund for the money to buy the Stardust in the first place.

I was less than a block away on Sherwood Street when Lefty's car blew up. The explosion was so loud the apartment actually shook. There was such commotion at Tony Roma's that I just decided to stay put.

About four weeks after Lefty's bombing, Gerri McGee Rosenthal died at 4 am in Los Angeles, in the lobby of the Beverly Sunset Motel at 8775 Sunset Boulevard. She had been hanging out with pimps and druggies, and she overdosed. However, many believe she was given a "hot shot" and murdered. Many believed that Frank had ordered it. Who knows?

Hughes Was Buying Up
LAS VEGAS

EVEN THOUGH HUGHES DIDN'T GET the Stardust Hotel and it went to the Mob, Hughes was still the biggest employer in the state of Nevada, and he did it without ever appearing before the county or state gaming commissions.

Hughes wasn't finished buying up Nevada, not yet. He added the Paradise Country Club to his collection, 200 acres of land in Paradise, Nevada; 150 acres right on the Las Vegas Strip; as well as a 25,000-acre ranch, including Warm Springs, a working cattle ranch. He even bought a laundry company. A laundry may not sound like much, but many of the smaller hotels and motels didn't have a laundry and sent out their bed linens to be washed every day.

But there was still that television problem. There were four television stations in Las Vegas in 1968: KLAS-TV (CBS), KORK-TV (NBC), KTNV-TV (ABC) and KVVU-TV (INDEPENDENT) and they all signed off the air around 12:30 am. Each station aired an 11 pm news program followed by a movie, and then they said "good night." Hughes felt that Las Vegas was a twenty-four hour town with twenty-four hour entertainment and should have a twenty-four hour television station, especially since he watched television all night. So in 1968, Hughes purchased KLAS-TV from the flamboyant, well liked, and respected *Las Vegas Sun* publisher Hank Greenspan for $3.6 million. He guarded it like a little boy guards his first bicycle; even Maheu didn't dare go near the place. In the years I worked for Hughes and KLAS-TV, I never saw Bob Maheu at the station. Every time I did see him, it was at the Hughes offices at the Frontier or at the Grand Opening of the Landmark Hotel ... just not at KLAS-TV. Now that Howard had his own TV station, he could watch his favorite movies all night long, and in many cases he did just that. And if he didn't like what was on the air, he would call the station and change the schedule. He never stopped a movie in the middle if he didn't like it, like people say. It just never played again.

Who Was Running the
HUGHES HOTELS?

BEFORE HUGHES GOT TO LAS Vegas, the hotels were either run by or owned by organized crime. Money was being skimmed to organized crime families in the amount of millions of dollars a day going to Chicago, Kansas City, New York, and Tampa. The owners or casino bosses would just go into the counting room, load up their attaché cases, and walk out. Who was going to say anything? They even rigged the money scales to give a phony weight, reading out a lesser amount, up to 40 percent less than the value of coins being weighed. So when Hughes came to town, popular belief was that he was going to run the Mafia out of town, but it was not true. Surprisingly, things changed very little with the advent of Howard Hughes. So who did Howard Hughes hire? You guessed it—the mob guys! Hughes needed people with experience to run a casino, and in Las Vegas most people with that experience were either in the mob or had organized crime connections. Two of the most profitable asinos in Las Vegas, the Hughes owned Desert Inn and the Sands, were losing money, but the mob guys were making out better than before. Remember, and this is important—those were the guys who knew how to get the money *out* of the counting room before it got *into* the accounting room.

The skim was in; it was a mob job. That's the reason that both the Desert Inn and the Sands were losing money. It was going out the back door as fast as it was coming in the front door, and the big guys knew it. So Hughes pulled out his Mormon overseers, who knew nothing about gambling and liquor, and allowed the mob guys to operate the Desert Inn and the Sands again. And bingo, they both became profitable again. But not for long. The mob was taking money out of the hotels almost as fast as the hotels were making it. The funny thing is Hughes didn't seem to care, or he didn't know—he probably didn't know. The losses weren't made public until after Hughes died.

Sinatra at
THE SANDS

THE RAT PACK, WITH FRANK Sinatra, Dean Martin, Sammy Davis Jr., Peter Lawford, and Joey Bishop, was a big draw at the Copa Lounge in the Sands Hotel. (The success of the movie *Ocean's Eleven* contributed to their popularity.) They always attracted the "high rollers" with big bucks, and they brought something else, which annoyed Howard Hughes. They brought the Mafia. The place was crowded from the time they arrived until they left. You couldn't even get a hotel room at the Sands. You would think Lucky Luciano, Frank Costello, and Vito Genovese were doing their version of *The Three Tenors*.

The Rat Pack attracted people like Sam "Mooney" Giancana, boss of the Chicago organization. Sam loved to spend time in Sinatra's dressing room with his girlfriend, Phyllis McGuire of the famous singing group, the McGuire Sisters. There was New York boss Carlo Gambino; New Jersey boss Angelo DeCarlo; Las Vegas boss Johnny

Roselli; former Chicago boss, Paul "The Waiter" Ricca; Paul "Skinny" D'Amato, owner of the famous 500 Club in Atlantic City and also one of the owners of a hotel in northern Nevada, The Cal-Neva. Skinny was a close friend and partner of Frank Sinatra. There were also Tampa boss Santo Trafacanti and Vinnie Albanese. Reportedly, Hughes never knew about it, but the "official" greeter of the Sands Hotel was none other than Charles "Babe" Baron, former Chicago gunman and a member of the Al Capone organization. Baron worked for Meyer Lansky and Santo Traficante in Cuba before coming to Las Vegas and the Sands Hotel. Up until the last days, the place was like a Who's Who of organized crime.

Every time the Rat Pack played the Sands, it made Hughes climb the walls. I don't think it was so much the fact that they were members of the Mafia that enraged Hughes but just the fact that he hated Frank Sinatra, and the feeling was mutual. In the '50s, Howard Hughes was in love with Ava Gardner. He bought her everything she didn't want or need. He got her jewelry, cars, trips to Europe on private planes, even movie parts. However, she fell in love with Frank Sinatra and married him. From that moment on, the battle lines were drawn. Howard couldn't stand Frank, and Frank couldn't stand Howard.

The Rat Pack headed by Frank Sinatra included Dean Martin, Sammy Davis Jr., Peter Lawford and Joey Bishop and appeared in the Copa Room at the Sands Hotel.

Hughes wanted to get rid of Sinatra at the Sands Hotel and didn't care what it cost him to lose "Ole Blue Eyes" and the Rat Pack. So he asked Bob Maheu to come up with a scheme to get rid of "The Chairman of the Board" for good and make Sinatra quit. Sinatra loved to gamble, his favorite game was blackjack, or 21. He would gamble away ten to twenty thousand dollars a night; if he lost, he would just sign a marker for more, up to $100,000 a night. So the hotel put a limit on Sinatra at $3,000 a night. When Sinatra learned of the limit, he went wacko and immediately went looking for Carl Cohen, the casino manager, not realizing that the orders came from much higher up. Sinatra spotted Cohen in the coffee shop. So he went to the back of the hotel, got a golf cart, and drove it through the plate glass window outside the coffee shop, screaming obscenities and anti-Semitic remarks at Carl Cohen. Carl walked to where Sinatra was, sitting in the golf cart. When he saw Carl, Sinatra jumped from the golf cart and hit Cohen with a right hook. This quite possibly was Sinatra's biggest mistake. Francis Albert tipped the scales at a mighty 152 pounds and measured in at towering five feet seven inches. On the other hand, Carl Cohen just happened to be a collegiate boxing champion. He stood six feet five inches and weighed in at better than three hundred pounds. It was kind of like Mike Tyson against PeeWee Herman. Cohen answered Sinatra's hook with a right cross that knocked two teeth out of the Chairman of the Board's mouth and set him on his ass. Sinatra's bodyguards were all there and saw the whole thing, but after watching Carl slug the Chairman, not one of Sinatra's bodyguards, including Sinatra's pal Jilly Russo, intervened. It seems they were smarter than Frank. Frank flew back to LA, had a little dental work done, and stayed there for a year or more. When Frank returned to Las Vegas, he played Caesar's Palace exclusively.

When the hotel and casino employees heard about it they were thrilled; they even had signs printed saying, "Cohen for Governor." Sinatra was very high maintenance; he was very demanding and bullied many of the employees. One night a busboy walked by Sinatra's table carrying a tray full of dishes. Sinatra stuck out his foot and tripped the busboy. Sinatra and his friends laughed, thinking it was hilarious. As the bus boy got up from the floor, I guess Sinatra felt a little guilt about the whole thing, so he threw the busboy a black and white chip worth a hundred dollars. The bus boy threw the chip right back at Sinatra, hitting him on the cheek. He told Sinatra to go and f**k himself and walked off. Nothing else was made of the incident.

Carl Cohen was a very well-liked boss at the hotel and probably one of the best casino managers in Las Vegas, if not the best. When the show that my sister Eleanor Sheridan was skating in at the Aladdin Hotel closed, she was offered a job as a cocktail waitress at the Sands, which actually paid more with tokes (tips) than the skaters were making. It was there she got to know Carl Cohen. She ultimately ended up as one of, if not the first, female bacara dealers on the Strip. The job paid a tremendous amount of money. In the 1970s, some dealers were making six-figure amounts. One night my sister made a $5,000 tip from a billionaire called Adnan Kashogi. She dealt him some good cards, and he walked away with nearly a million dollars profit.

Eleanor said Carl Cohen was loved and respected by the employees of the Sands. If there was ever a problem, you could always go to Carl, and the problem was gone. Carl Cohen and Jack Entratter, the entertainment director, sold the Sands to Hughes, and the both of them stayed on as employees. Entratter was the owner of record of the famous Copacabana Night Club in New York City. However, the real owner was mob boss Frank Costello, boss of the Commission. Jack Entratter knew almost everyone in the national media, as well as most of the entertainers who worked for him in New York. Entratter owned 12 percent and Carl Cohen owned 9.5 percent. There were many other owners, or partners, as they preferred to be called. Some were owners without the blessing of the Nevada Gaming Commission. One owner was Abner "Longey" Zwillman, a New Jersey mobster, who, with Johnny Roselli and Anthony' Tony" Accardo, put the deal together for Harry Cohen to purchase Columbia Pictures, including the signing of Marilyn Monroe to a two-picture deal.

Frank Sinatra: movie star, singer, friend of presidents and gangsters. He was the leader of the Rat Pack and an Oscar-winning talent (12/12/1915–5/14/1998).

NACHO GARCIA

*Jilly Rizzo was a restaurateur, a friend
of Sinatra's, and his bodyguard.*

Sam "MoMo" Giancana was the "Boss of Bosses" of the Chicago Outfit. He was put there by Frank Netti, Paul Ricca, and Anthony Accardo (6/15/1908–6/19/1975).

*Marilyn Monroe, known as a famous movie star and
girlfriend of the Kennedy brothers (6/1/1926–8/5/1962).*

Sammy and the
X-RATED VIDEO

SOMETIME IN 1969, I WAS shooting commercials for Hughes Air West with Norm Crosby, Wayne Newton, Sammy Davis Jr., and Joey Bishop. The shoot went well, and afterward Sammy Davis Jr. asked me if I would make him copies of the commercials. We only used two-inch tape in those days, and Sammy said he would provide the tape for the dubs. I told him it would take us a couple of hours, but we would be happy to do it. I told him I would call him at the Sands when it was completed. Sammy returned with the blank two-inch tape and left it with the video engineer. Minutes later, engineer Alvin Zuckert, who later became an Emmy-winning director, came over to me and said, "You better take a look at the tape Sammy dropped off. It's all hard core porno." I looked at it, and it was enough to make Linda Lovelace blush. I called Sammy at the Sands and told him what was on the tape. He acted very surprised and told me he didn't know how something like that could ever get on his tape. I asked him if he wanted us to record over the porno. He again denied any knowledge of the porno and told us to record over it. The guys at the station wanted to keep the porn on the tape, so they dubbed it to another tape and labeled the porno "Church Reel," knowing nobody would look at it with that label. So Sammy got his commercials, and the engineers got Sammy's porno.

NACHO GARCIA

Sammy Davis Jr., a great entertainer and a member
of the Rat Pack (12/8/1925–5/16/1990).

*Joey Bishop, comedian and last living member
of the Rat Pack (2/3/1918–10/17/2007).*

Hughes Couldn't SAY NO TO a Pretty Face

IT'S BEEN SAID THAT HOWARD Hughes's biggest love in life was aviation. That's what people thought, but I think it was his second-biggest love, in spite of holding five world aviation records, building the biggest plane in the world, and owning the second-largest air force in the world during the making of the motion picture *Hell's Angels*. His biggest love was women.

"The Old Aviator" held more records with women than he did with planes When Howard Hughes owned RKO Motion Picture Studios in Hollywood, it was like putting a little boy in charge of a candy store. Howard believed the old adage that "Too much of a good thing, is a *pleasure*," and that's the way he lived his life. He just couldn't resist a pretty face and didn't even try.

Howard Hughes never missed an opportunity to discover a star. He was the Galileo of the silver screen. Hughes dated just about every big star in Hollywood, including Ava Gardner, Rita Hayworth, Faith

Doumergue (Do-Meer), Susan Hayward, Jean Harlow, Katharine Hepburn, Ginger Rodgers, Jean Simmons, Liz Taylor, Jean Peters, Terry Moore, Lana Turner, and many, many more. He even married two of them (Jean Peters and Terry Moore). He started living with one of them when she was only fifteen years old, with her parents' permission, which was still illegal. Her name was Faith Doumergue (Do-Meer), and after a long romance with Hughes, Faith married Teddy Stauffer of restaurant and frozen food fame. Another actress, the beautiful Rita Hayworth, was so mad at him for not wanting to get married, she aborted their love child at the American Hospital in Paris, France. It would have been Hughes's only child. Two famous actresses, Bette Davis and Linda Darnell, both left their husbands for Hughes.

BIANCA OLIVAS

Katharine Hepburn, Hughes's first love, in
Hollywood (5/12/1907–6/29/2003).

*Jean Peters, a star at 20th Century Fox in the 40s and 50s and
second wife of Howard Hughes (2/3/1918–10/17/2007).*

Howard Hughes and Ava Gardner.

*Faith Domergue lived with Hughes when she was
only fifteen years old (6/16/1924–4/4/1999)*

Terry Moore, actress, says she married Hughes in the 40s. (1/7/1929)

Jane Russell, star of "The Outlaw"
(6/21/1921 to 2/28/2011)

Hughes caught syphilis from a very famous actress at that time, an American sweater girl. That really freaked him out. He burned all of his clothes and got rid of all of his expensive cars and never associated with the girl, who shall remain nameless, again. From that time on Hughes only bought black Chevrolets, with one exception—a special airconditioned Chrysler New Yorker with an aircraft air filtration system that took up the entire trunk. Much of Hughes strange behavior in later years could possibly be attributed to the tertiary stages of syphilis. Hughes was first treated for syphilis by Dr. Vern Mason, in Los Angeles. His son, Dr. Vern Mason Jr., is still in LA.

Hughes always referred to the sweater girl as his "Sikorsky Baby," in memory of the times they had sex on the floor of his Sikorsky airplane as it flew on auto pilot over Los Angeles at 14,000 feet … Can you imagine doing that today, with all the air traffic?

I was working at Channel 9 in Los Angeles, now KCAL-TV, and a woman from the news department asked me if I worked for Howard Hughes in Las Vegas. I said I had, and then she told me the following story:

In May of 1953 Hughes was reading *Life* magazine and noticed the girl on the cover. She was a stunningly beautiful girl from Indiana—just the type Hughes liked. For weeks he couldn't think of anything else. So he sent an RKO talent scout to Indiana to meet Sallilee Conlon and her mother. Hughes flew them to Las Vegas, where he wined them and dined them and took them to every show in town. This went on for three months. Hughes finally offered Conlon a studio contract. He set Sallilee and her mother up in a home in Coldwater Canyon. He arranged for singing, dancing, and acting lessons five days a week. Sallilee said the arrangement was strictly platonic and nothing of a sexual nature ever happened between them.

So she told me, and I believe her. Hughes would take her out every week or two, to a movie premiere or dinner; then he would become involved in a business conversation with other producers or aviation people, and he would have one of the Mormon aides drive her home. Weeks became months and months became years, and after five years Sallilee decided to move out and enter the real world again.

Sally entered the television news business, and when I met her she was a producer for George Putnam. At that time, George was the number one anchorman in Los Angeles. I thought the world of George; he was a true and trusted friend. He had a ranch in Chino, California, and raised race horses. George even named one of his horses Sheridan. Sheridan looked great, but he was no Man of War. I'm not sure if he ever won a race; on second thought, I *am* sure—he never won a race. Sallilee took in one stray dog after another, just like their close friend, singer/actress Doris Day. Both women loved animals and couldn't stand to see them abandoned, so they gave them a home.

George had married years earlier and had two daughters. One day I asked George why he just didn't get a divorce and marry Sallilee. He said in his big, thundering basso profundo voice, "My God, Johnny, it would cost me millions. I'll just continue to give her money every month and let her have the house in Beverly Hills." Sallilee and George became partners and lived together for forty-plus years at The Putnam Ranch in Chino, California. The last few years of George's life he had a radio talk show in Los Angeles.

George passed away in 2008. There will never be another George Putnam, and for that, the media will never be the same. George was spontaneous, accurate, and exciting. He was the number one newsman in Los Angeles for years and the anchorman who Ted Knight, on the *Mary Tyler Moor Show* in the 1970s, patterned his Ted Baxter character after.

Hughes Did
ABSOLUTLY
Nothing for Her

YEARS LATER, IN 2008, IN Las Vegas, I met one of Hughes's lawyers, Paul Wynn, who started working for Hughes as a telephone operator on Romaine Street in Los Angeles, working under Frank William (Bill) Gay, Howard Hughes's chief Mormon. Paul Wynn went to law school at USC in Los Angeles and became a lawyer for Hughes. In the short time I knew Paul, I found him to be honest and truthful. Wynn knew Sallilee Conlon and her parents and told me, "It's a tragedy what Hughes did to Sallilee." I asked him what Hughes did to Sallilee, and Paul replied, "*Nothing,* absolutely *nothing.* She had the singing voice of an angel, comparable to Jane Powell or the late Katherine Grayson—maybe even better than both of them. Hughes put her under contract. He paid for her acting, singing, and dancing lessons, her home and transportation. He even had her cut a record with the great Maestro Bakalienakoff of motion picture and symphony fame. "It was superb, I don't think I ever heard better, and I know because I've heard it several times," said Paul Wynn. But Hughes never did a thing for her career, and that was a tragedy." Because she had an overabundance of talent.

After a while, Sallilee felt that Hughes wasn't going to help her in the entertainment business, so she and her mother moved out of the house Hughes got for her. She looked for other horizons, working in television. She was lucky in that field. When I met her, she was working as a producer in the news department at Channel 9 in Los Angeles, at KHJ-TV, now known as KCAL, a CBS-owned station. At that time Channel 9 was owned by RKO Pictures, which had been owned by Howard Hughes.

Hughes wasn't finished with women, not yet. What people don't know is that Hughes had over one hundred—I know it's hard to believe; but he had over a hundred women sequestered around Hollywood in apartments and rented homes. This is no joke—he had over a hundred women just waiting for him to call.

None of these girls was allowed to have a boyfriend. They had to be available twenty-four hours a day, and they had to follow a strict schedule of lessons and occasional dinners with Hughes. Hughes's aides were watching the girls most of the time and reporting back to the boss. However, none of the girls ever made it to the big time. After a few years Hughes could no longer keep up with the demands of a hundred girl friends. So he sold RKO Studios and moved on. Remembering that too much of a good thing is a *pleasure*, Hughes kept a few actresses under contract at his new offices at the Samuel Goldwyn Studios.

There was a time when Hughes fell for a working actress. Her name was Vera Ralston. Hughes fell in love with her the first time he saw her; he provided her with a car and one of his Mormon drivers. Hughes wanted to put her under personal contract, but she kept putting him off. What do you think happened? Vera Ralston and the Mormon driver Robert Miles fell in love. They ran away and got married. Hughes was so upset that he told the head of the drivers, Bill Gay, that from then on he was to only hire homosexual drivers, but that never happened. There was another actress named Vera Ralston, a former skater with the Ice Capades. Her husband thought he could make another Sonja Henie out of her. She was the wife of the owner of Republic Pictures, Colonel Herbert Yeates. The only problem was she couldn't act. So, the other Vera took her new husband's name and became Vera Miles, a favorite actress of director Alfred Hitchcock. One look at Vera, and you'll know why Hughes fell in love with her. In no time at all, Vera became an A-list actress.

Howard's Tryst in
THE DESERT

O N December 29, 1967, Hughes decided to fly up to the Cottontail Ranch, a legal house of prostitution near Goldfield, Nevada, in Lida Junction. Hughes wanted to visit a girlfriend named Sunny, who worked at the ranch; that is the only name she was known by. We don't know where Sunny is today, or even if she's alive, but, we know Hughes had known Sunny since 1953, when her then boyfriend was the MC at one of the hotels on the Strip, the El Rancho Vegas. Sunny was a blonde with a diamond encrusted in her top left incisor. Howard knew Sunny for fifteen years or more.

Hughes called Bob Deiro, an executive with Hugh Airports in North Las Vegas. He instructed Deiro to meet him at the airport and get ready for the 160-mile flight to Cottontail Ranch. Bob knew Hughes and had flown him to Ash Meadows a few times, another house of prostitution, as well as The Cottontail Ranch. As a matter of fact, Bob flew Hughes all around Nevada to check on his mining claims and to look at property in Goldfield, Tonopah, Coaldale, and Silver Peak, Nevada.

Tonopah, by the way, is the town where Hughes married actress Jean Peters. Popular belief has it that they were married in the Mizpah Hotel, but that's not true. Howard married Jean in room thirty-three at the L & L Motel, in Tonopah, Nye County, Nevada, on January 12, 1957, under factious names:

Howard Robard Hughes was G. A. Johnson of Las Vegas. Jean Peters was Marian Evans of Los Angeles Walter Bowler was the justice of the peace, Tonapah, Nevada. James Perry and D. Martin Cook were witnesses. D. Martin Cook was a Hughes employee; however, I was unable to identify James Perry.

Howard Robard Hughes (9/25/1905–4/5/1976)

*Jean Peters; a star at 20th Century Fox in the 40s and 50s, and
second wife to Howard Hughes (02/03/1918–10/17/2007).*

MARRIAGE CERTIFICATE

STATE OF NEVADA, } ss.
COUNTY OF NYE.

N° 5130

This is to Certify that the undersigned Walter Bowler
did on the 12th day of January A.D. 19 57 join in lawful
Wedlock G A Johnson
of Las Vegas State of Nevada
and Marian Evans
of Los Angeles State of California
with their mutual consent, in the presence of James Perry
and D Martin Cook who were witnesses

Walter Bowler

JUSTICE OF THE PEACE
TONAPAH, NEVADA
(Sign this in official capacity)

Witnesses:

TO BE GIVEN TO THE RECORDER

No. 5130
Filed for record at request of
Wm. P. Beko, Dist. Atty.,
May 27, 1957
at ___ minutes past 2 o'clock
___ m and recorded in Book ____
of Marriage Certificate s ____
page _____
Nye County, Nevada Records
County Recorder

Hughes/Peters marriage license

At the Cottontail
RANCH

HUGHES HAD BEEN TO THE Cottontail Ranch numerous times. He knew Beverly Hurrell, the madam and owner of the ranch. She knew who Hughes was, but none of the other people knew Hughes, except "Sunny." Beverly Hurrell kept Howard's secret until the day she died, telling only her husband. She said she thought about going public with the information, but she had decided against it. She said she was worried about her own safety. Not so much because of Hughes, but because of Moe Dalitz, Johnny Roselli and their other friends … Capice?

Hughes and Diero arrived about 8:10 in the evening. It was cold and already dark. Hughes went in to see Sunny, and, to keep out of the cold, Bob went to the kitchen for something to drink. Whether Sunny and Howard were dancing the "coital ballet," or whatever they were doing, was their business. Howard suffered from such germ phobia that I find it hard to imagine he was doing the big number. But again, that was their business.

Well, it was warm in the kitchen all right, and after a couple of beers Bob dozed off. What had only seemed like minutes turned into a few hours or more. A woman entered the kitchen and asked Bob if he was the pilot. He said he was, and he was told his passenger returned to Las Vegas with another customer. The first thing that went through Bob's mind was, "I'm *fired*." As it turned out, Hugh never said a thing to Bob about what happened that night.

Hollywood got into the Howard Hughes biography business with a motion picture called *Melvin and Howard* in 1980. The story was quite accurate, but nobody believed it at the time. However, it didn't do much for Melvin's reputation. It made him look foolish. *Melvin and Howard* was a very good motion picture, directed by Jonathan Demme, a great director. *Melvin and Howard* won two Oscars, one for best original screenplay and another for best supporting actress (Mary Steenburgen). The motion picture starred Jason Robards (a distant cousin) as Howard Hughes and Paul La Mat as Melvin Dummar. In the movie, as in real life, Melvin claimed he was left 1/16 of the Hughes estate, according to the Mormon Will. Melvin Dummar said Hughes promised him that Hughes would remember Melvin's kindness.

About four hours had passed since Hughes met Sunny at the Cottontail Ranch. He returned to the plane looking for Bob Deiro, but Bob wasn't there. Bob was a sleep in the kitchen, but Hughes didn't know that. On his way back to the Cottontail Ranch, Hughes was asked by a customer if he was going to Las Vegas, and Hughes said yes. The man offered Hughes a ride, and Hughes accepted. They got about one and a half miles from the ranch before the man stopped the car. He beat Hughes up and took his money—about $8.00. Hughes hardly ever carried any money. The robber took a cheap wrist watch and kicked him out of the car on the side of the road. At that time, Hughes was in his sixties, six foot five inches tall, and weighed 105 pounds. He was not in very good condition and was lucky he lived.

Nobody knows how much time went by when Melvin Dummar came driving by. He had to relieve himself, and he pulled over to do just that. There were no gas stations or restaurants in that area, and when you have to go, you pull over and you go. Melvin looked to his right, just off the road, and saw a body. He thought it was a dead man. He went over to check, and he heard the man groan. Melvin pulled the man to his feet. He was cold and had cuts on his head and abrasions on his face. At first Melvin thought the man was an old derelict, but he wasn't about to leave anyone out in the desert. Melvin was told what happened, and the man asked Melvin to drive him to Las Vegas. Melvin couldn't leave the man out in the cold in winter weather. So he relented and headed to Las Vegas. He was on his way to Los Angeles and had to go through Las Vegas anyway. Melvin's new friend didn't talk much on the way to Las Vegas, other than to say he had recently moved to Las Vegas and was visiting a friend at the Cottontail Ranch. Then he asked Melvin his name and wrote it down. Hughes asked Melvin what he did for a living, and Melvin said he was self-employed.

Hughes said he would never forget the kindness Melvin showed him. Then he said, "My name is Howard Hughes." This just added to Dummar's suspicion that his passenger was living in a world of delusion. They arrived in Las Vegas, and Dummar dropped Hughes off at the Sands Hotel. A security guard noted the arrival and license plate number, but only because Dummar was driving a dented 1966 Chevrolet Caprice, and the Sands was a pretty up-scale place, with Lincolns, Rolls-Royces, Bentleys, and Mercedes Benzes in the driveway; a '66 Chevy seemed out of place. Hughes actually lived at the Desert Inn, but he owned the Sands, the headquarters for Frank Sinatra and the Rat Pack, as well.

The Cottontail Ranch was located in a very rural and isolated location called Lida Junction, about fifteen miles past the town of Goldfield. Beverly Hurrell, the madam, had a tough time recruiting girls, because none of them wanted to live that far away from big towns like Las Vegas or Reno, both of which have laws against prostitution. Though the house had its own airport to fly in customers, it didn't seem to help, except in Hughes's case, and that was because he had his own plane. After many recruitment and marketing problems, the Cottontail Ranch closed its doors in the early 2000s. However, in late 2003 the ranch was purchased again. The new owners hoped that with an influx of investments, advertising, and a website, it would attract new working girls and especially customers. They hoped it would be open for business on a more permanent basis. But just as before, in the spring of 2005 the Cottontail Ranch, without new girls, again fell upon hard times, and it has been closed ever since. In 2011, the Cottontail Ranch was still up for sale, at an asking price of a million dollars.

Cottontail Ranch

Cottontail Ranch

Cottontail Ranch airstrip

Melvin Dummar: possibly saved Hughes's life

Howard Was Becoming
A LAS VEGAN

BY 1968, HUGHES WAS REALLY becoming a part of Las Vegas. He hired attorney Tom Bell to make the right political contributions to Senators Cannon and Bible, Congressman David Towell, Governor Paul Laxalt, DA George Franklyn, and Sheriff Ralph Lamb, as well as the local judges, county commissioners, and JPs.

Howard was busy watching his new toy, KLAS-TV, and making changes to the programming. He hated most of the commercials that were played on *Swing Shift Theater,* a segment of the all-night programming actually created by Hughes. That was the time period between 1 am and 3 am, after the *Merv Griffin Show* on CBS. Hughes especially hated one commercial, called the Adjusta-Bed spot. He found it annoying, misleading, and poorly produced. So he decided to pull it off the air. Tom Bell, his Las Vegas attorney, told Hughes he would open himself up to a lawsuit if he interfered. So Hughes didn't pull the spot. He just limited the number of times the commercial could be played on *Swing Shift Theater*. Television air time was cheap at that time of night, and the Adjusta-Bed people had a big advertising budget, so they ran between eight and ten spots in a two-hour time period. There was, however, another client who played almost as many spots as the Adjusta-Bed people. But we never heard a peep out of Hughes about them—not a peep. The client's company was called Carnaby Street, and their fare was sexy women's clothing and lingerie. Carnaby Street had four or five beautiful Las Vegas showgirls modeling their clothes—in some cases the lack of them. Carnaby Street stayed on the air in Las Vegas for many years. Those commercials weren't quite as popular with the viewers as they were with some of the crew members.

Howard rarely went to bed until about 9 am; one reason for that was *Romper Room*, a children's program that aired live each morning. The host of *Romper Room* was a beautiful woman named Jimmie Lou Adam, and Hughes loved beautiful women. He watched the show daily; her character name on the show was Miss Barbara. If Howard had ever ended up with ABC, I'm sure Miss Barbara would be hosting *Good Morning America* today. However, Hughes never met Miss Barbara in person. He just admired her from across the street at the Desert Inn in his Barcalounger.

Beside the Adjusta-Bed commercials, which annoyed Hughes to no end, there was another program he couldn't stand and tried to have removed from the air. It was called *Sunrise Semester*. It was a CBS network program that came down on the network line that KLAS-TV was contracted to air five days a week. The problem was that CBS needed the show to fulfill its educational commitment to the FCC, and it couldn't be removed. So Hughes had to live with the Adjusta-Bed commercials, as well as *Sunrise Semester* on CBS.

KATCHO GARCIA

Miss Barbara from Romper Room, *real name Jimmie Lou Adam. She was Hughes's favorite on KLAS-TV*

It Was a Movie with
A...*BULLET*

ABOUT 1968, I RECEIVED A call at home about three in the morning. It was Paul Stoddard telling me to go to the studio and pick up a package from a Hughes Air-West pilot. So I went to the studio. Gary Marlow was the technical director on duty that night, and I waited for the Hughes Air-West guy. A little after 3:30 am, there was a knock on the control room door, and there was a pilot, carrying what looked like a sixteen-millimeter movie box. He asked me my name; I told him, and he handed me the box. I asked him if he wanted me to sign for it, and he said no. He said, "I gave it to you. You know it and I know it. That's all that matters," and he left. I thought that was a rather stupid remark, but I didn't say anything. I looked inside the box, and there were two sixteen-millimeter movies in it. One was *The Long Hot Summer* and the other was a brand new movie called *Bullet*, with Steve McQueen. I thought Mr. Hughes wanted to see them in the privacy of his penthouse, because both movies were still in general release. As a matter of fact. *Bullet* had just opened at the Marilyn Parkway Theater on Marilyn Parkway and Charleston Boulevard. I didn't think much more about them. I took them home with me and brought them back to the studio in the afternoon to preview them and make sure there was no black or academy leader in the film. There wasn't, so I put them away and waited for further instructions from Hughes.

A couple of nights later, at about 10:30 pm, before the news, I got a call from Hughes on the "hot line." He asked if I got the films that were sent over by Hughes Air-West, and I told him I had. He told me he wanted to see *Bullet* after the news, on the air. I told him Merv Griffin was on at that time. In 1968, NBC had Johnny Carson, ABC had Dick Cavett, and CBS had Merv Griffin. I said were obligated to play Merv, and I asked him if he wanted me to pre-empt Merv. He said, "No, play it after Merv." Gary Richey, another director, was in the studio at that time, and because I was on the phone for so long, he began to mark the news scripts for me.

As soon as the news was over I called the station manager to let him know what was going on, but I couldn't reach him. Bob Maheu was not available, so I called Paul Stoddard. He was number two to Maheu. I told Stoddard that I got a call from Howard Hughes. I was pretty sure it was Hughes, because he was hard of hearing and had what sounded like a thousand cycle tone, an amplifier, on his phone. Anyway, I just wanted to make sure it was really Hughes before I did what he wanted me to do. I didn't want to risk the license of the television station on a prank phone call. Stoddard said, "I'll call you back in five minutes." In less time than that, he called me back and said he spoke with an aide at the penthouse and was told Hughes had called the station. So it was Hughes. I asked Stoddard if he wanted to know what Hughes wanted, and he said, "No, I really don't want to know."

I said, "Okay. You'll read about it tomorrow in the newspapers."

Then he said, "Oh, hell, what did he want?"

I told him, "Hughes wanted me to play *Bullet*, with Steve McQueen, at 1 am, right after the *Merv Griffin Show*, while *Bullet* was still playing in general release."

Stoddard said, "Thank you, Johnny," and just hung up.

About 12:30 am, I walked into the control room and told Gary Marlow, the technical director on duty, "Here is what were going to do, and this comes from the Old Man. Were going to play *Bullet* right after *Merv*, without commercials."

Gary looked at me like he was just hit in the face by an Ampex quad tape machine and said, "Is he *nuts*, or what?" So, at exactly 1 am., Las Vegas got to see its first first-run motion picture on television, even before the networks had a chance to show it—Steve McQueen starring in *Bullet*. It would have never happened anywhere without Howard Hughes.

Shit hit the fan in the morning, with phone calls from Cleveland Amory from *TV Guide*; Roy Neal, *NBC News*; Terry Drinkwater, *CBS News*; and people from the *Dick Cavett Show* from ABC-TV. They all wanted to know the same thing: Was Hughes using his television station as a video recording machine for himself? I told everyone the same thing … I was home in bed and didn't know anything about it. Actually, I had gone up to the Flame, a bar and restaurant about 150 yards west of the station, on Desert Inn Road and the Strip, with Ted West, an engineer at the station. It was a hangout for media types, entertainers, and show kids from the Strip, as well as some of Hughes's people, like Tom Bell, Paul Stoddard, and Channel 8 people, like Chuck Russell, Gary Richey, Tom Foy, Alvin Zuckert, and Don Baile. Also included were Brendan Boyer of the Royal Irish Showband; Brendan O'Brian of the Irish Dixies, occasionally Mel

Tome from the Sahara, Liberace from the Rivera, and others who were in strip shows.

Believe it or not, the same thing happened a couple of weeks later with *The Long Hot Summer*. I'm not sure what the result of that was, but whatever it was, Hughes stopped playing new movies on the air at night. Everything that happened was always a secret, so it was pretty hard to find out anything. I was told that Hughes was fined, as well as charged with violations of the copyright statutes and misuse of intellectual property, all amounting to around $200,000—peanuts to America's first billionaire.

GTT, or Grand THEFT TAXIE

QUITE A FEW FUNNY THINGS happened during my time at KLAS-TV.

I can't believe I'm revealing this, and I have no idea what got into me, but here it is: One night Chuck Russell, Channel 8's weatherman, and I were walking in the rain up to the Flame Restaurant and Lounge, about 150 yards west of the studio, for an adult beverage. A taxi with its motor running was parked right in front of the door. So we had to squeeze past the cab and the wall to enter the restaurant, getting even more wet in the rain. Chuck said, "Ya know, someone should steal that cab for being parking that way and teach that dumb-ass cab driver a good lesson."

"I said, "You don't have the stones to do it.""

My friend said, "You don't either."

"Bet me," I said, and with that I jumped into the cab and took off. I couldn't believe what I'd just done. Chuck went on into the bar, still not believing what he'd witnessed. I drove the cab into the shopping center at the Strip and Convention Center Drive. I was thinking, *There's a good chance I may be recognized getting out of this cab at a busy shopping center on the Strip, in front of a well-known deli like Mr. Sy's directly across the street from the Stardust Hotel.* But nobody recognized me, thank God. On the way back to the Flame, on foot, I passed a hotel swimming pool and tossed the cab keys into the pool. As I walked through the bushes to the Flame parking lot, I could hear yelling and swearing. I saw the very large cab driver standing outside the Flame, in the rain, with his bewildered passenger. He was in a state of panic and delirium. I said, "What's the matter?" and Chuck said, "Someone stole this guy's cab."

Then I said, "Who would steal a cab?" and the cab driver said, "That's what the fu-k I want to know. Who would steal my fu--ing cab?" Everybody in the Flame knew exactly what happened, and years later, every time I would walk into the Flame, the bartender, Bill La Russo, or Ed Jaffee, the owners, would yell out, "Taxi!" Las Vegas was a small town then, and I'm surprised the cab driver never knew who stole his cab, because just about everyone else did.

Elvis at the
ALADDIN

IT WAS ABOUT THAT TIME in 1968 that my sister Eleanor, my brother Denny, and my girlfriend Mary were skating in the ice show at the Aladdin Hotel. So I drove Mary up to the hotel for the midnight show. I intended to watch the show, but I stopped at the small bar east of the casino to visit with my friend Ernie, the bartender. It was a great little lounge, with wonderful entertainment most of the night. There was the Great Tommy Deering Trio with Jerry Zapata and Dodie Ruffin. Joey Dero's Group was there five nights a week, and they were an eleven on a scale of ten. I don't know exactly how this happened, but security came in, in force, and for some reason they ignored me. All of a sudden, I found myself standing next to Elvis Presley and his four body guards. I was never a big fan of Elvis Presley, even though I thought he was better than most rock & roll artists. Elvis introduced himself to me and asked me if I was a local who lived in Las Vegas and what I did there. I told him I worked for Howard Hughes, as well as his TV station, and that did it! Elvis wanted to know all about Hughes: what did he look like? Did he only hire Mormons? Did he have a harem of women at the penthouse? Was he a Republican? I told Elvis I never saw Hughes in person and that I talked with him occasionally on a secured phone line at the TV station, and I knew little about his personal life.

Elvis looked into my eyes and said in his Southern accent, "Johnny, you lie like a rug." I just couldn't convince him I never saw Hughes in person. We talked about a million things: karate, guns, the police. He was a reserve deputy sheriff in Shelby County, Tennessee, and showed me his star. He talked about the upcoming television show he was about to do and seemed really excited about it. His main interests that night were Howard Hughes, television, and law enforcement.

Little Richard was the guest headliner in the show my sister, brother, and girlfriend were in at the Aladdin Showroom, and Elvis wanted to see him. However, he never made it to the show; nor did I. Eleanor, Denny, and my girlfriend Mary showed up after the midnight show was over; it was already 2:30 am. We had been talking about three hours. About three years earlier in 1966 my sister was skating with "Holiday on Ice," a show not unlike Ice Capades. It was in Memphis, and Elvis had invited the entire cast to Graceland. He talked with my sister about that party and the ice show in general and how he always wished he could skate, and then he said, "Tell your brother to tell me the truth about Howard Hughes," and she just laughed.

All of a sudden a really big guy pushed his way through security and walked up to our table. He threw a hundred dollar bill on the table in front of Elvis and said, in a very aggressive manner, "Elvis, I want you to sign this to Barbie. Write 'Love ya, Barbie. Elvis'." Just then two giant security officers came toward the man, as well as

Presley's own bodyguards, when Elvis raised his right hand. Elvis said, "Sir, I'd be happier than a pig in you-know-what to sign that bill for your little lady. I hope y'all are having a great time tonight." I couldn't believe the change of attitude in that man. He profusely thanked Mr. Presley, as he called him. He shook hands and thanked the bodyguards and casino security; he turned around and walked back into the casino. Then Elvis looked at security and his guys and said, "Boys, that's how you do it." I was just amazed at Elvis. He never had a drink, never had a cigarette, and never uttered a swear word. A little while later Elvis asked us to join him for dinner in the Saber Room the next night. He told my sister to invite as many people from the show as she wanted and to invite Little Richard and his people, as well. That night about twenty-five people showed up for the dinner. The show kids left for the show check-in, and I stayed with Elvis for about an hour more. Finally he had to leave, he planned to see Brendan Bowyer and the Irish Showband at the Stardust Hotel, the next night for sure. Brendan did a great impression of Elvis, and Elvis wanted to see it. I can tell you this—I never met a nicer person in all of my life. He was definitely a prince among men. Now I know why they call him the *King*. It's funny, but Howard Hughes and Elvis both loved the Aladdin. I don't know why Hughes loved it so much, but I know why Elvis loved it—it's where Elvis got married, in the Saber Room.

Mary Howard, John Harris Sheridan, Elvis Presley, Eleanor Sheridan

Danny Mahony
COULD HAVE
Been Sheriff

T HERE WAS A COP FROM the Las Vegas Metropolitan Police Department named Danny Mahony. Danny had a great personality, and everyone at the station liked him. He was kind of a professional Irishman, and you couldn't help but like him. He even had a little lapel pin he wore on St. Patrick's Day that said, "If you're not Irish, you ain't Shit." So we decided to make him even more popular in the community. At least once or twice a week we would do a little story about Danny Mahony on the weather. We even promoted him to sergeant. We referred to him as Sergeant Mahony so much that people started to call him Sergeant. Then Danny took the test and was promoted to sergeant for real. A few months later we decided to promote him to lieutenant. We would do a story like this: "Lt. Danny Mahony from the Las Vegas Metropolitan Police Dept. asks that if you are driving in the rain tonight to please drive safely, because the life you save … may be his." Finally the sheriff, Ralph Lamb, called the station and asked us to stop promoting Danny on the air. Well, he actually made lieutenant and we stopped.

About 12:30 am on March 16, the night before St. Patrick's Day, Danny and two or three of us from the station were painting the center line down Las Vegas Boulevard North green for St. Patrick's Day. (We used water-based paint that would wash right off.) We were right in front of Magahey's Irish Bar, in North Las Vegas. The Nevada State Highway Patrol saw us painting the yellow line green, and their red and blue lights came on. They stopped us, but when they recognized Danny (Lt. Mahony) with a paint brush in his hand, they said, "Happy St Patrick's Day, Mahony," and got back in their police cruiser and drove off. Danny Mahony retired from the police department and was elected to the city commission. He's still living in Las Vegas.

The Wolfman Comes
TO SIN CITY

ONE DAY I GOT A call from "Wolfman Jack." He was a
very popular disc jockey heard nationally. The Wolfman
broadcasted from a powerful radio station in Mexico, so the FCC
or other government agencies couldn't tell him what he could do on
the air. He would sell autographed pictures of Jesus and the twelve
Apostles at the Last Supper over the air. He was very irreverent, but
sometimes funny. Well, the Wolfman wanted to talk to me about
doing a show with him on television. We had one meeting, and I got
a call from the sheriff asking me not to do a show with the Wolfman.
He said the Wolfman would bring the wrong type of people to Las
Vegas. He said he was sure Hughes wouldn't want that type of person
on his television station and that he was going to send someone to
talk to the Wolfman. I don't know what that meant!

In those days, other than the Mafia, the most powerful person in
town was the sheriff. Not only did he run the police on the Strip but

the work cards, the cards that allowed a person to work in a casino or could deny that person the privilege. The sheriff was also the chairman of the Clark County Gaming Commission, which licensed all of the hotels and gambling casinos on the Strip. So, when the sheriff asked you to do something, it was more of an order—because next to the governor of the state of Nevada, the sheriff of Clark County was the most powerful politician in the state.

Move over Leonard Goldenson, HERE COMES Howard Hughes

HUGHES LOVED HAVING HIS OWN television station. He loved it so much he decided to buy the ABC television network. Howard offered $74 a share for the stock, which was selling for $58 at that time. The people at ABC were very concerned about it, because they knew of Howard's propensity for never making up his mind and for changing things at the last minute. To put it bluntly, the big-wigs at ABC were scared as hell. The president of ABC, Leonard Goldenson, did everything he could to block the sale. He asked the stockholders not to approve the sale. He filed suit in federal court, saying the sale violated FCC laws, as well as federal antitrust laws. Howard said he had no intention of getting involved in the artistic content being aired by the network. He said he felt he could bring it up to par with the other two networks, because of his company's technical knowledge. He already owned Hughes Sports Network, which produced sports shows, like the Dina Shore Golf Championships, from the Desert

Inn Hotel and Country Club. However, Leonard Goldenson of ABC wasn't about to give up on his network. He took double truck ads out in the *New York Times* and other newspapers accusing Hughes of trying to buy ABC-TV at an under market value, not just below the stock value. Goldenson said ABC was worth much more than the stock indicated. Goldenson also said Hughes was making deals with senators and others not to appear before the FCC in person to answer their questions. That was true. But just when it looked like Hughes was going to get the ABC television network, Hughes backed out of the deal.

Howard Hughes wanted the network for the political power he would hold by owning one of the Big Three networks. However, he wasn't about to face the press, ABC's Leonard Goldenson, and the FCC in his present condition. So he stayed up in the ninth floor at the Desert Inn on his Barcalounger and watched another episode of *Hawaiian Eye* and *Swing Shift Theater*.

KLAS-TV in LAS VEGAS

MY JOB AT THE STATION was to direct the five, six and eleven o'clock news, but I was also in charge of Hughes's films. I think because I was a film editor at my former job at KOOL-TV, now Fox-owned and operated Channel 10 in Phoenix. I think I just fell into the job. The VHS videotape recorders we know today weren't around in 1968, so everything I sent Hughes was on sixteen millimeter film. His favorite television shows were *Sundance,* with Wil Hutchens; *Maverick,* with James Garner, Jack Kelly, and Roger Moore; *77 Sunset Strip* with Efrem Zimbalist Jr., Roger Smith, and Edd "Kookie" Burns; *Hawaiian Eye,* with Robert Conrad, Anthony Eisley, Connie Stevens, Poncie Ponce, and Tiko Ling; *Run for Your Life,* with Ben Gazzara; and *Cheyenne,* with Clint Walker. Each day I would write a synopsis of the shows and movies he wanted to see, with a list of the stars, the directors, and the releasing studio and send it to him at the penthouse. Sometimes he would change his mind and call the studio or have an aide call the studio to change a movie we had scheduled to run. Indecision from the penthouse seemed to be the only course of action, in those days.

Sonny Liston and Moe **AT THE DESERT** *Inn Coffee Shop*

MOE DALITZ WAS SITTING IN the Desert Inn Coffee shop having a little lunch, and in walked Sonny Liston. Sonny had just lost a fight to Leotis Martin. Sonny always lied about his age; he claimed to be thirty, but he was really thirty-eight. During their conversation Moe brought that up. He said, "Sonny you're not as young as you used to be, and I know how old you really are. Why don't you just give it up?" For some reason that really irritated Sonny, and he let off with a barrage of anti-Semitic and other insulting remarks. Then he looked at Moe and said, "Moe, I'll kick your ass." That was not a very smart thing to say to Moe Dalitz. You never wanted to mistake Moe's kindness for weakness, and Sonny may have learned that the hard way. Moe looked at Sonny and said in a very deliberate, but soft voice, "Sonny, if you do, you better kill me, because I'll pick up this phone and you'll be dead in twenty-four hours." Sonny had a hunch that Moe was not kidding. So he made an about-face and left the Desert Inn, never to return.

On December 5, 1970, Sonny Liston was found dead on the floor of his living room under strange circumstances. His wife Geraldine found his body in their Las Vegas home.

In the book *Boxing Babylon: Behind the Shadowy World of the Prize Ring*, *Ring Magazine*'s editor in chief Nigel Collins wrote about Liston's tragic life and strange death. Many sports writers believe Liston was murdered, given a drug "hot shot," meaning someone put a gun to his head and someone else injected him with an overdose of drugs. But it looks like what killed Sonny will remain a mystery forever … Yea!

*Sonny Liston, former world champion boxer (Birth
date unknown, Death 12/30/1970)*

Morris Barney 'Moe' Dalitz, born in Boston, MA: bootlegger, racketeer, casino owner. He shaped Las Vegas into the modern city it is today. (12/25/1899–1/15/1983)

Johnny, Sam
AND MARILYN

JOHNNY ROSELLI HAD AN OFFICE and an apartment at the Desert Inn Hotel. He met Hughes at the train when he arrived in Las Vegas, but he never laid eyes on him. He was instrumental in Hughes getting the Desert Inn Hotel. That doesn't make much sense to me, but that's what happened. Roselli worked for and was a friend of Mafia boss Sam "Mooney" Giancana of Chicago. It was Sam who ordered Marilyn Monroe killed. I know it's hard to believe, but I believe. Chuck Giancana, Sam's brother, and I heard it many times from Las Vegas wiseguys. Monroe was killed by the use of a "hot shot." According to Chuck Giancana, in his book *Double Cross*, Sam ordered mob members from Kansas City and Detroit, under the supervision of two Mafiosi named Giaonla and Torterella, to kill Marilyn and to kill her with the knowledge and approval of the Central Intelligence Agency because Marilyn threatened to go public about her affairs with the Kennedy brothers, John and

Bobby. Unlike Liston's hot shot, Marilyn's was a hot shot of Nembutal and a combination of barbiturates and chloryl hydrate. They used a suppository because it would enable the medication to be absorbed quickly through the anal membranes directly into the bloodstream, and it left no needle marks. It was a perfect weapon to kill Marilyn. And the world thought she overdosed on her personal drugs. It was hard to tell exactly what type of drugs she ingested, because after the autopsy her stomach was missing. The LA coroner was Dr. Thomas Naguchi, and her stomach was missing. Marilyn was murdered!

Job security as a La Cosa Nostra boss or a Godfather has its drawbacks. Sam Giancana, along with Johnny Roselli and Santo Trafficante, was to testify before a Senate Select Committee on his knowledge about the CIA's involvement in the attempted assassination of Fidel Castro and probably John F. Kennedy. However, before he could appeared before the committee, Giancana was found shot to death in his home in Oak Park, Illinois, before he was to testify.

He was shot once in the head, once in the mouth, and five times under the chin, with a .22-caliber pistol, which is a favorite assassination weapon of the CIA and the Mafia. Was it a mob hit or was it a CIA hit? Only a few people know for sure, and they're not talking. The mob thought Sam Giancana was talking too much and violated the La Cosa Nostra Oath of Omerta (mafia-silence), and the CIA was afraid of having its involvement in the death of Marilyn Monroe found out, as well as their involvement in the assassination attempt on Castro. As well as any involvement they may have had in the assassination of John F. Kennedy. So who did it? Oswald!

Johnny Roselli, born Filippo Socco: the mob's man in Los Angeles and Las Vegas. Had ties with the CIA. (7/4/1905–8/9/1976)

Sam "Mooney" Giancana was the "boss of bosses" of the Chicago Outfit. He was put there by Frank Netti, Paul Ricca, and Anthony Accardo. (6/15/1908–6/19/1975).

Marilyn Monroe murdered in her BelAir home.

The Benefits of Mafia
EMPLOYMENT

ROSELLI WAS FOUND, HIS LEGS chopped off and his body chopped up, in a fifty-five gallon drum floating off the coast of Florida. He was killed to cover the conspirators' tracks. Whether it was the CIA or Mafia or both, the killers are not known. But someone for sure wanted to keep Roselli quiet. Many believe Trafficante was behind both the Roselli and Giancana murders. The connected guys think Roselli was ordered to kill Giancana, and afterwards Trafficante had Roselli killed to keep him quiet. Isn't it strange that the gun that killed Giancana came from Florida, Trafficante's domain Was it just a coincidence? Do cows really fly?

Sam Giancana, boss of bosses, Chicago Outfit

Johnny Roselli

Santo Trafficante, Mafia boss of Tampa, Florida, and the Southeast USA. (11/15/1914–3/17/1987)

Here is an interesting note: Chuck Giancana, Sam's brother, in his book *Double Cross*, says that just a week prior to his death, Sam "Mooney'" Giancana placed a contract, rumored to have been requested by a former president or by the CIA, on Jimmy Hoffa. The job was given to five soldiers: two from Chicago, one from Boston, one from Detroit, and one from Cincinnati. One month later Hoffa did disappear. Sam Giancana always said, "Find out who is alive and you'll find the killer." Giancana was gone, Roselli was gone ... Bingo—Santo Trafficante was the only one to survive.

Who was Johnny Roselli, and why was he so important in the Hughes organization? The only people who would know the answers are Howard Hughes, Bob Maheu, Paul Stoddard, and Tom Bell, and they are all dead. Maybe a few Hughes aides would know, but they're not talking either. In the early years, Johnny got involved with the Chicago Mafia, working for Al Capone. He was sent to Los Angeles by Anthony Acardo to look after the Mobs multi-million dollar extortion plot against the motion picture industry. With Mafia money, he helped Harry Cohen to gain control of Columbia Pictures. Johnny Roselli, Abner "Longey" Zwillman, and Tony Accardo ended up with a small piece of the studio. In the 50s, Roselli became more and more involved in Las Vegas but still kept his Los Angeles interests. In the 60s Roselli was drafted by Bob Maheu, former FBI agent, CIA operative, and chief executive officer of Hughes Nevada Operations, to put together a group to kill Castro. Roselli introduced Maheu to Sam Gold (real name: Sam Giancana, Chicago Mafia boss) and a guy named simply Joe. (Joe was Santo Trafficante, the Tampa Florida boss and big casino owner in Cuba.) The assassination attempt was later cancelled, by the White House.

In the '60s Sinatra got Roselli a membership in the Friar's Club, a private club for wealthy show business members. Roselli learned of an elaborate cheating operation, with hidden cameras, engineered by Murray Friedman, a Las Vegas friend of Roselli's. When he learned of the scam going on, Roselli told Murray that from then on they were partners, and half the money would go to Chicago. In 1967 the scam was discovered by the FBI, and Friedman and Roselli were arrested. Harry Karl was one of the big losers at the Friar's, loosing millions of dollars, including his home, family, and wife, Debbie Reynolds. The other losers included singer Tony Martin; Jack Benny; Zeppo Marks; producer Joe Schenk, actor, Phil Silvers; and producer Louis B. Mayer. Roselli was eventually convicted and fined $55,000.

However, Roselli still had his place at the Desert Inn Hotel and Country Club and his business there as well: the Monte Presser Agency, where he represented many of the big showroom productions, acts, and stars, with a percentage of that money going to the Chicago Outfit.

This is *funny* ... Roselli was deported back to Italy in 1968, but Italy refused to accept him. So he stayed in Las Vegas, doing occasional jobs for Maheu and Hughes and killing for the CIA or Mafia or both. You had to remember—no matter how nice Johnny Roselli was, he was a major killer.

It's been said by former Chicago hit men that Johnny Roselli, Charles "Chuck" Nicoletti, Marshall Caifano (who was replaced by Johnny Roselli in Las Vegas), along with James Files, aka Jimmy Sutton, that Roselli fired the fatal shots that killed President John F. Kennedy, on the orders of Sam "Mooney" Giancana and Carlos Marcello.

The son of Joseph Bonanno, boss of New York's Bonanno family, Salvatore "Bill" Bonanno said in his book that Johnny Rosseli told him while they were both in prison that he, Roselli, fired the shot from a storm drain on Elm Street, in front of the Texas Book Depository in Dallas, that killed President John F. Kennedy. Remember, Johnny Roselli doesn't lie, except to judges and cops.

This was how Chicago and organized crime kept its hand on Las Vegas: Johnny Roselli was sent to Las Vegas by Tony Accardo; Marshall Caifano was sent to replace Johnny Roselli when Johnny was indicted on gambling charges in the 60s. Marshall Caifano was sent by Sam Giancana. Marshall Caifano was replaced in 1971 by Tony Spilotro, who was sent by Joey Auippa; Don Angelini was sent to replace Tony Spilotro in 1985 by Joey Auippa, after Spilotro and his brother Michael were beaten with shovels and bats and buried alive in their underwear, as portrayed in the movie *Casino*." The boss now is very quiet.

A Little Competition
FOR HUGHES

KIRK KERKORIAN SHOWED UP IN Las Vegas with $100,000,000 in cash in his pockets, from the sale of his charter airline service Trans International Airlines, and he bought the Flamingo Hotel and Country Club. Hughes took notice of it, but that was all. He wasn't worried about competition from Kerkorian, not yet anyway. A while later Kerkorian announced to Las Vegas and the world that he was about to build the biggest hotel in the world. This did cause Hughes a little trepidation, because he had plans for building the biggest hotel in the world, the four-thousand room Super Sands.

Kerkorian had his hotel almost completed; it was called The Las Vegas International, now known as the Las Vegas Hilton, on Paradise Road and Convention Center Drive. Hughes owned the Landmark Hotel, right across the street from Kerkorian's Las Vegas International Hotel. The Landmark was nowhere near as big as the International, but it was the tallest building in Nevada at the time. It was a strange-looking building, with what looked like a flying saucer on top of it. It was originally built by Frank Carroll, who ran into money problems, and the hotel sat vacant for years. Hughes bought the hotel and decided to open it the same day as Kerkorian planned on having the grand opening for the Las Vegas International. KLAS-TV, Hughes's station, was scheduled to shoot the opening, but we never knew when the opening was going to be, because Hughes kept changing dates. First it was to open the same day as the International; then it was changed to the day before; then to the day after; and finally back to the same day as the Las Vegas International opened. But then as the day approached, Hughes changed his mind again. Who was Hughes going to get for the opening? He was driving Maheu crazy. He thought of reuniting the Rat Pack. But he hated Sinatra, and Sinatra hated him, so that was out. Maheu kept looking for name talent, because Kirk Kerkorian had signed Barbra Streisand as the act to open the brand new Las Vegas International. Hughes didn't like Barbra Streisand's politics, so it didn't bother him that Kerkorian signed her. He thought about Dean Martin, but Dean Martin and Frank Sinatra were friends, and he didn't think Dean would do it. So he offered him a couple of movie parts and Bingo. Dean Martin decided to do it, along with Bob Hope and Danny Thomas. Well, a couple of days before the grand opening, Bob Hope cancelled because of a death in the family. From that time on, Hughes never again spoke to Hope. Maheu kept submitting a guest list to Hughes, only to have all the names rejected. Finally Hughes approved forty-five or fifty names, and Maheu invited another three hundred, including Johnny Roselli and friends.

Barbra Streisand

KLAS-TV, the Hughes television station covered the grand opening of the Landmark Hotel for about an hour. It may have been longer, but after forty-plus years I can't quite remember. On the other hand, the opening of the new Las Vegas International was covered for about two minutes. I don't think that was a directive from Hughes but an ass-kissing tactic on the part of the station manager and news director.

I believe one of the reasons Maheu had such a hard time getting an opening date and other information from Hughes was Hughes's heavy drug use. One of the sad reasons Hughes couldn't make up his mind and would then change it so often was his drug problem. Hughes's use of drugs was increasing at this time, especially his use of codeine; he was even starting to shoot it. He used Emprum-4 when he couldn't get codeine; his use of Blue Bombers also escalated.

Hughes was using massive amounts of valium, as well. He was taking eight to ten times the normal amount. Hughes had two MDs on staff; wouldn't you think they could have done something to help Hughes? Maybe they just didn't want to. Maybe they thought that if Hughes just died, they would be taken care of. Some say his drug use was to ease the pain from his 1946 plane crash into actress Rosemary DeCamp's home, which almost cost him his life and caused Hughes great back pain ever after. But his doctors should have known better. I think they did and just didn't care.

In 1968 Hughes had a blood transfusion, ordered by his cardiologist, Dr. Harold Feikes of Las Vegas. The transfusion was probably a detoxification method due to his heavy drug use. He told his doctor and his aides that he wanted only Mormon blood and absolutely no Negro blood, and he wanted the names and addresses of all the donors. Then before he took one drop of the blood he had the donors all investigated for drug and alcohol use, as well as their sexual habits. He even wanted to know what they ate. God help any Mormon who ate fried chicken, chitlins, or water melon.

Howard and
JIM CROW

HOWARD WAS NOT BORN IN Houston, Texas. He was born in Humble, Texas (pronounced: Um-ble), on September 24, 1905, not December 24, 1905. That was during the Jim Crow era. He always mistrusted "coloreds," as he called them, and I can't think of one who worked for him in a management position. He just didn't want to be around them. Howard suffered from "Afro-phobia." Hughes used to preview all of his movies at the Sam Goldwyn Studios in Hollywood. It was a small room, big enough for his Barcalounger plus a smaller one for his wife Jean Peters. The studio provided security. It was an ideal place for Howard. Then one day he learned that producer/director Otto Preminger was using his screening room during the day to watch rushes of *Porgy and Bess*. *Porgy and Bess* had, with a few exceptions, an all-black cast, and that set Hughes off. He told his aides, "Can you imagine coloreds being in this room, sitting in my Barcaloungers and watching a movie? That Otto Preminger character even cheats on his wife with Dorothy Dandridge." Hughes then ordered his Barcaloungers burned and moved to another screening room on Sunset Boulevard. I doubt that the Barcaloungers were really burned, but Hugh thought they were, and that's all that mattered.

On another occasion Hughes was watching the competition, KSHO-TV, the ABC affiliate in Las Vegas; the show was *The Dating Game* with Jim Lang. One of three women was to be chosen for an all-expense-paid European vacation on TWA Airlines. Then Hughes noticed the contestants were "two black women and one beautiful white woman" (Hughes's words). This time there was a twist in the selection process. The man's eight-year-old child was to make the choice. After the questioning period, the child chose the white girl to go to Europe with his father, a black man. That set Hughes off again. What added to his fury was the fact that they were going to Europe on his airline, TWA. He said this was done for no other reason than shock value. Then he said, "That's it—I don't want ABC anymore." Then calm hit the penthouse again after Hughes learned that the white girl was actually a light-skinned black woman. Her name was Alice Jubert, an actress who starred with Lou Gossett Jr. in *J. D.'s Revenge*. She played Senator Heart's secretary in *Friday Foster* with Pam Grier, Godfrey Cambridge, Ertha Kitt, and Jim Backus. She played herself on the *Richard Pryor Special* with John Belushi.

The Afro-phobic bug bit again on April 20, 1969. Hughes decided to watch the Tony Awards. He shouldn't have done that, because the award for Best Play went to *The Great White Hope*, a story about an interracial romance between a black boxer and a white woman. Jane Alexander (the white woman) won for best supporting actress, and James Earl Jones (the black man) won for best actor. That put Hughes in a bad mood for weeks.

Bob Maheu was a real sports guy, and he loved boating and

tennis—he loved all sports. So he arranged to have the Davis Cup come to Las Vegas. It would be a real coup, a brilliant stroke. When Hughes found out, he was pleased, until he learned that Arthur Ash would be competing, and he was black. So Hughes ordered the Davis Cup cancelled. He told Maheu he didn't want the Desert Inn full of "coloreds." He said, "Tennis is not a game that appeals to those people anyway." I guess in the late 60's Hughes couldn't have heard of the sisters, Serena and Venus Williams. Maheu then told Hughes that if he cancelled the tennis matches Howard could have his resignation. Hughes thought about it for a few minutes, and the matches went on as scheduled.

Maheu really took a big chance with Hughes. He was making $10,000 a week. That's over half a million a year in 1967 money. Plus Hughes gave him two Cadillac cars and a yacht he kept in La Jolla, California; he also bought him a $500,000 mansion on the Desert Inn golf course.

Howard Hughes as he looked in his final years.

Robert Maheu, chief executive officer: Hughes Nevada Operations.

Hughes and
PAUL HARVEY

H OWARD WAS HAVING DINNER ONE night, his normal steak, peas, and ice cream. He had that almost every night, along with his favorite ice cream, strawberry with pralines. He was watching the news on Channel 8, KLAS-TV, and Paul Harvey popped up. Paul Harvey had a show where he commented on everyday events and closed with a short editorial. Well, Norm White, the general sales manager, thought he could sell the show in Las Vegas and asked Mark Smith, the station manager, to buy it. So Mark bought it. Under normal circumstances that's the way things work—in a normal television station. However, Howard was running the station from his bedroom, and nobody asked him if they could change the format of the news. And Howard wanted Paul Harvey off his television station. Not that he disagreed with Paul Harvey's opinions, because he didn't. But since he wasn't asked for his opinion, he wanted Paul gone. So he told Paul Stoddard to see if Channel 5 wanted the show or to sell it to any other station. If he couldn't sell it, he was just putting it in the station library and would pay off the two-year contract. And that's what happened.

Burton Cohen, another Las Vegas icon, loved by people who knew him or worked for him, the president of the Desert Inn Hotel, learned that they were running out of Hughes's favorite ice cream (strawberries and pralines). So Burton called the penthouse for instructions. John Holmes was on duty at the desk and was told they don't make that ice cream anymore; if they wanted more they had to order three hundred gallons. Knowing Hughes loved that ice cream, John told Burton to go ahead and order it. The ice cream arrived at the Desert Inn ten days later, and as if Hughes was behind it all the time, Hughes said, "Ya know, John, I don't think I want that strawberry ice cream with pralines anymore. I think I'll have chocolate from now on." Well, they hardly had enough room to store three hundred gallons of ice cream in the kitchen of the Desert Inn. Since Hughes wasn't eating it anymore, they gave it away free to all the dinner customers. I ate there a couple times a week, and I actually heard a waitress say, "Sir, the hotel would like to give you a complimentary dish of ice cream for desert." I got some of that ice cream, and I can see why Hughes quit eating it.

Hughes Out
AND ABOUT

HUGHES WAS SEEN MANY TIMES, at many locations, by many people. He was known to take trips with his Mormon aides to McCarren Airport and North Las Vegas Airport to watch the planes take off and land. This is very strange, but a friend of mine who was a Hughes aide swears that it happened, and he was there. Hughes went to see the show in his own hotel at the Desert Inn called PZAZZ; he saw George Arnold's "Nudes on Ice" at the old Aladdin Hotel, a favorite hotel of both Hughes and Elvis Presley. It was the hotel where Elvis married his wife Priscilla. Hughes visited the Lido de Paris at the Stardust Hotel, Casino de Paris at the Dunes, and Folies Bergere at the Tropicana Hotel. These were the greatest shows that ever played the Las Vegas Strip and now are gone forever, a real tragedy for the changing town, replaced by cheap nickel-and-dime topless reviews, with very few exceptions. Logistically, getting ready for Hughes to attend shows like those unseen was a nightmare. He always entered late and left early, sometimes arriving in a wheelchair His table would be in the back, and four aides would enter first. A few minutes later Hughes would enter with two or three other aides.

These aides, although not personally known to the public, were known in Las Vegas as the "Mormon Mafia." For some reason that moniker made Hughes smile. Murray Westgate, Hughes's favorite television anchorman in Las Vegas, said Hughes was asked why he always had Mormons with him, and he replied, "They live a clean life, they're good family men, they don't smoke, they don't gamble, and they don't drink. People who drink become somebody else, and they're not the people I hired in the first place." Murray Westgate anchored the 6 and 11 pm news on Hughes's television station, KLAS-TV. Many times Hughes was busy doing something else, so he ordered the 11 pm news to be videotaped and played back again at 2 am. So this became standard operating procedure, another television first.

Who saw Hughes in Las Vegas? With the exception of his Mormon aides? Hughes's airport executive Bob Diero, who flew Hughes to the houses of prostitution in Central Nevada, as well as trips to Tonopah and Reno to look at his mining interests—Diero obviously saw Hughes. Hughes was seen by Governor, later Senator, Paul Laxalt; Governor Michael O'Callaghan; and quite possibly Sig Rogich, former ambassador to Iceland and president of Rogich Communications in Las Vegas; Sig was very instrumental in Ronald Reagan's election. Beverly Hurrell, the madam of the Cottontail Ranch, saw him on many occasions. Hughes met Anastasio Somoza, president of Nicaragua, and the US ambassador to Nicaragua, Turner B. Sheldon; Sunny, who worked at the Cottontail Ranch; Melvin Dummar, who picked Hughes up in his car on the highway outside the Cottontail Ranch; a few showroom captains, who probably didn't know who he was; Desert Inn security; a few hotel bosses; a show producer and showroom orchestra conductor Hank Shank and a lighting director. I'm not saying they all even knew who he was. But to say Hughes was sequestered away on the ninth floor of the Desert Inn Hotel is like saying Hughes danced in "Boylesque" on weekends on the Strip.

Bye-Bye, LAS VEGAS

IN LATE 1969, HUGHES WAS seriously considering leaving Las Vegas. His attempts to stop the atomic testing were falling on deaf ears. He was concerned about the water supply and what was happening to it from that testing. He hired Larry O'Brien, from the Kennedy organization. He told O'Brien, "Do whatever it takes," including putting money in the right hands to stop the testing. Twice Hughes sent Robert Maheu to Washington, with a million dollars in cash, to secure promises from Lyndon B. Johnson and later Richard Nixon to end nuclear testing in Southern Nevada. But Nixon was paranoid about taking any money from Howard Hughes. In 1956, Hughes lent $200,000 to Donald Nixon, the president's brother, which was never repaid. When knowledge of the loan became public in 1960, Nixon believed it cost him the election with John F. Kennedy. Many believe that Hughes disliked Nixon so much that he deliberately leaked this information to the media. He did, even though he disliked Joe Kennedy, the president's father, more.

Also, Howard was becoming uncomfortable with Bob Maheu. But this was by design—Mormon design. Frank Gay and Kay Glenn, the two top Mormons, as Hughes called them, wanted Maheu out. So they made Hughes feel like Bob Maheu had been letting Hughes down and was untrustworthy, even stealing, in relation to the nuclear testing program, the grand opening of the Landmark in Las Vegas, the ABC-TV deal, and so on. Gay had mistrusted Bob Maheu, and he was jealous of him and the power Maheu wielded as chief executive officer of Hughes Nevada Operations. Frank Gay asked Hughes to have Maheu investigated time and time again, but it always fell on deaf ears. Gay ordered Hughes's aides to make it difficult for Maheu to contact Hughes. Gay, Davis, Holliday, and Henley were worried about Maheu's perceived power and that the power Maheu had was eclipsing theirs. So it became a power struggle between the people at Hughes's tool company in Texas and Hughes Nevada Operations in Las Vegas. The Hughes aides were in a very powerful position. They determined who would talk with Hugh on the phone and whose mail would reach Hughes; they would make sure Hughes heard unflattering, misleading, and outright libelous reports about Maheu and those they didn't approve of or those who their bosses didn't approve of: bosses like Frank Gay, Chester Davis, and Raymond Holliday. They were in a position very similar to Martin Borman, who had determined who could contact Adolf Hitler and who couldn't. Frank Gay, especially, told the aides to withhold messages to Hughes from Bob Maheu and Jack Real and others he considered a threat to his own position.

Hughes Leaves
LAS VEGAS
for Good

HUGHES LEFT LAS VEGAS FOR good the night before Thanksgiving 1970. It was a quick operation, in the planning stages for more than a year, and it was run with military precision. The Hughes aides strapped Hughes to a stretcher and carried him down the back stairway, which was the inside fire escape of the Desert Inn, down nine stories to the Desert Inn parking lot to a waiting van. The aides put Hughes into the van and headed north on Las Vegas Boulevard and south to Nellis Air Force Base, where Hughes had three airplanes waiting. Two were decoys; only one, the Lockheed Jet-Star, would carry Hughes and his Mormons to Nassau, the Bahamas.

When the people at Hughes Nevada Operations (HNO) and KLAS-TV learned of Hughes's departure, they went absolutely ballistic. Even secretaries from the HNO office at the Frontier acted as though they were in the know and in charge. But nobody knew who was in charge. Nobody wanted to choose the wrong side. It was rumored that Robert Maheu had been fired, but he said he was still in charge. It was asserted that Hank Greenspun, Maheu's pal and publisher of the *Las Vegas Sun* was helping to create the confusion by printing articles implying that Hughes was kidnapped or ill. One headline read, Hughes Vanishes, Mystery Baffles Close Associates. This just added to the uncontrollable unrest throughout the state of Nevada. Hughes sent new people to Las Vegas to take over Hughes Nevada Operations. Raymond Holliday, Frank Gay, Chester Davis, and Nadine Henley, all from Hughes Tool Company in Houston, Texas. Frank Gay, who Hughes referred to as his "Chief Mormon," was from Los Angeles, the old Hughes office at 7000 Romaine Street, Los Angeles, but he was with that group.

Still, the Hughes people didn't know who to take orders from. Was Maheu still the boss or were the Texans in charge now? Hughes tried to clear up the situation with a phone call to Governor Paul Laxalt from Nassau, the Bahamas. Laxalt received a call from Hughes on December 7, 1970, confirming that Hughes had fired Maheu. Now Then it was clear to all that Hughes Nevada Operations had new leadership—the Texans.

Maheu sometime later told the *Las Vegas Review-Journal*, "I know who is driving the train, and it's not Howard. It was Bill Gay and Chester Davis of the so-called Mormon Mafia."

This was not a good time for Hughes. His "Afro-phobia" was starting to kick in again, because the Bahamas was then run by a black man, Prime Minister Lyden Pindling, who granted Hughes special privileges, such as entering the country without a valid passport, work permit, or investment in the country. However, the opposition party started to question Hughes's aides and wanted entrance into Hughes's suite at the Britannia Beach Hotel. That was as much as Hughes could take, so he rented a boat and headed for the Florida Keys.

Managua and the Intercontinental Hotel was the next stop for Hughes. It was the best hotel in Managua, shaped like a pyramid, and Hughes occupied the biggest suite in the hotel. Presidente Generalissimo Anastasia Somoza made it clear to Hughes through U.S. Ambassador Shelton that he would have no problems in Nicaragua. He welcomed Hughes with open arms. He just needed Hughes to invest in his bankrupt National Airlines of Nicaragua—the airlines which El Presidente owned. In light of that and to show good faith. Hughes bought 25 percent of the airline's stock. But that didn't satisfy Somoza. A pharmaceutical company and real estate company were next on El Presidente's wish list. There was the Samoza plywood company that needed a little financial infusion, as well ... and so it went. Late in December 1972, a massive earthquake hit the city of Managua, killing more than five thousand people. Hughes left for Florida the next day, after spending his last night in Managua at the presidential palace. He was glad to get out of Managua and away from El Presidente, who was beginning to cause him some concern.

Ooooooh
CAN...A...DA...

VANCOUVER, BRITISH COLUMBIA, CANADA, WAS next on the itinerary. He loved Canada and stayed there for six months, at the Bayshore Hotel. When he arrived, he astonished his Mormon aides by walking through the hotel lobby and talking with strangers. He would sit down with them and begin long conversations with people he never met. His aides were trying their best to get him to go up to his suite, but he was having too good a time. Then he decided he wanted to go outside to the marina and walk along the docks, look at the different types of boats, and just look at the ocean. I think they reminded him of the time he and Katharine Hepburn spent on the East Coast, sailing off the Connecticut shore. He stared out at the water for what seemed like an eternity but in reality was only a few minutes. Finally the Mormon aides were able to get him up to his suite. They put him in his Barcalounger, darkened the room, and provided him with his "medication." In no time at all, he slipped into a drug-induced haze that would hold him prisoner and make him easier to manage. In the six months he was there, Hughes secretly left the hotel three or four times to drive along the ocean and see the city. One of the aides told me Hughes was probably the happiest in Vancouver, happier than any place he had been since leaving Las Vegas. The people looked like Americans, they were polite, they spoke English, and he could watch American TV. What more could you ask for? Hughes loved Canada and its people. However, when the tax people started checking into his residence status, it was time for him to hit the road again.

Clifford and
HIS PAL HOWARD,
Who He Never Met

IT TOOK A BOOK TO get Hughes ambulating again. He was hopping mad. The book, *The Autobiography of Howard Hughes*, written by Clifford Irving, was a complete farce. Irving was paid almost a million dollars by the publishers, McGraw-Hill. Irving claimed to have written the book after many meetings with Hughes, but Hughes never met or talked with Irving. It was all a scam. So on June 7, 1972, Hughes decided to clear the air with a national press conference. Involved was a panel of well known reporters, who either knew Hughes or had interviewed him in the past. They were: syndicated columnist James Bacon; Wayne Thomas of the *Chicago Tribune*; Vernon Scott, of the United Press International (UPI); Roy Neal, NBC News; Gladwin Hill, *New York Times*; and Marvin Miles, *Los Angeles Times*. When asked about Irving, Hughes said, "I don't know him. I never saw him, I never heard of him, until a few days ago, when this thing was brought to my attention." When asked about Maheu, Hughes said, "He's a no-good, dishonest son of a bitch who stole me blind." Maheu filed a seventeen and a half million dollar lawsuit against Hughes for libel and slander and added that amount to the fifty million dollars for wrongful dismissal. Maheu was ultimately vindicated, and Clifford Irving passed go and went directly to jail.

Hughes Wants
TO FLY AGAIN

SOMETIME LATER, HUGHES, WITH THE help of the Rothschilds, found himself in London, at The Inn on the Park Hotel, over looking Buckingham Palace. His drug use was getting worse, and his hands were shaking, but he decided he wanted to fly again, and that's exactly what he did. He flew a Hawker-Siddeley 748 over London. A man in his condition, strung out on drugs, very hard of hearing, with very poor eyesight who refused to get glasses, was flying an airplane with passengers over one of the world's most populated and famous cities. The night before he made his "first" flight over London, Hughes jumped onto his Barcalouncer and watched airplane movies. His Mormon aides had already bought him new flying clothes, including a new Stetson fedora hat. He had his hair cut to look presentable to his co-pilot, Tony Blackman, an Englishman. On a Sunday in June 1973, he flew out of Hatfield Airport, just north of London.

What happened next shocked even Tony Blackman, a veteran

pilot. Hughes jumped into the pilot's seat of the Hawker-Siddeley 748. It makes absolutely no sense to me, and I'm sure it makes none to you, either, but Hughes stripped off all of his clothes except for his Stetson fedora, grabbed the controls, yelled like a cowboy, and took off into the air. Hughes was accompanied by his good friend and Hughes executive Jack Real, Mormon aide Chuck Waldron, and test pilot Tony Blackman. He flew for more than three hours. Hughes would never have made the G best-dressed list in his famous Stetson fedora. Blackman was later quoted as saying, "It was the most bizarre experience of my aviation career. flying a Hawker-Siddeley 748 with an American billionaire in the nude." Hughes made three more flights, each lasting three hours or more, but they were to be his last. Hughes said that those four flights were the happiest times he had spent in many, many years. He purchased three of the Hawker-Siddeley planes for $2.6 million. The old Howard Hughes resurfaced, if only for a short time; but Jack Real said he saw the old Howard Hughes come alive again.

A few days after his third flight, Hughes was headed for the bathroom. He fell and fractured his hip. He refused to accept medical care and remained bedridden; his condition deteriorated, and his drug use increased.

Hughes flying over London, in the nude … with a hat!

Hughes Returns TO ACAPULCO

HUGHES DECIDED TO RETURN TO Acapulco, Mexico. One reason was the drugs were easier to get there. That's what the aides told Hughes, anyway, but it wasn't true. In actuality, location made no difference, because the drugs were ordered from a manufacturer in the United States. However, the aides wanted to live in Mexico, because Mexico was closer to their homes in Utah and Nevada than England was. This was just another way Hughes was manipulated by his aides for their own convenience, not for his.

When Hughes was running low on drugs, which was rare, and he had to get them locally, his doctors wrote prescriptions in the name of the Hughes aides who were purchasing the drugs and giving them to Hughes, eliminating a paper trail back to Hughes. Hughes hardly ate anything, and his weight dropped to ninety pounds. Wouldn't you think that would set off an alarm in his caregivers? They just didn't give a damn!

Hughes Gives His Aides a New Contract
AND RETURNS TO
Texas—Dead

A COUPLE OF YEARS BEFORE HUGHES died, the Mormon aides got a new contract with Hughes that would take care of them for the rest of their lives. Their salaries ranged from $120,000 to $150,000 a year in 1968 money. The new contract stipulated that after Hughes's death, they would continue to receive their salary for life, indexed to the cost of living, providing they never talked about Hughes or about his personal life. The aides would be paid as consultants; it would not be a retirement. A retirement cannot be stopped, but a consulting fee may be discontinued at any time, and that's exactly what Hughes intended to do if any of the aides talked. That agreement was almost tantamount to Hughes signing his own death warrant. I believe it was his death certificate. What motivation was there for the aides to keep Hughes alive? They could let him die and be home again with their families, receiving the same compensation as before but without having to take care for a drug-addicted old man.

Why was Hughes's major drug use not reported? Why was his

physical care neglected: his broken hip, his dramatic weight loss? At times Hughes was sometimes on the toilet as many as ten hours a day, or even more—shouldn't that tell his caregivers something was wrong? He was six foot four and weighed ninety pounds. What does that tell you? They all knew Hughes was addicted and did nothing except procure more drugs for him! It was almost as if they wanted him to die. I'm sure a few of them did. Not all, but certain aides treated him with contempt, disdain, and disrespect. They took advantage of everything Hughes had available. They would fly on Hughes's private plane from Acapulco to Florida for dinner on their days off or from the Bahamas to Florida for a stage show, all at Hughes's expense.

At six foot four and weighing ninety pounds, Hughes was almost dead. I'm guessing that only three aides cared. Most of the time, Hughes would stare into space, going in and out of a coma. His aides and doctors didn't know what to do with him, except for his Acapulco doctor, Dr. Victor Manuel Montemayor, who wanted to hospitalize Hughes at once, which quite possibly would have saved Hughes's life. But the Mormon aides nixed the idea. They were afraid to take Hughes to a Mexican hospital because of legal problems that could arise if Hughes died there. They just knew they had to get Hughes out of Mexico. Finally, at a little past noon April 5, 1976, the Mormon aides loaded Hughes onto a Graf jet with pilot Roger Sutton and co-pilot Jeff Abrams, doctors Thain and Chaffin, and aides John Holms and Chuck Waldron. At 1:27 pm, somewhere over Brownsville, Texas, the Aviator (Hughes) died in an airplane over his home state of Texas, headed for Houston. Howard Robard Hughes was seventy years old.

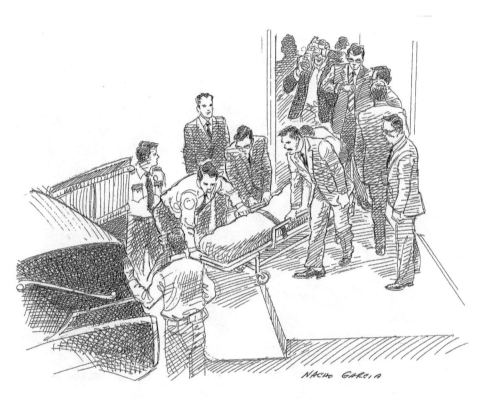

Hughe's body being taken out of the Methodist Hospital

The family says good-bye

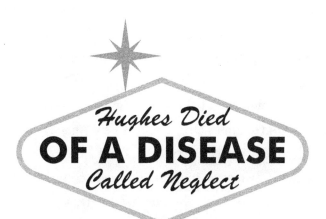

Hughes Died OF A DISEASE Called Neglect

THE CAUSE OF HUGHES'S DEATH was said to be chronic kidney disease, but the Mexican doctor who treated Hughes in Acapulco, Dr. Victor Manuel Montemayor, said it best: "Howard Hughes died an unnecessary death. In my opinion, he died from a disease called *neglect*."

Robert Maheu, when asked about the Mormon Mafia and Hughes's health care, responded, "If sheer neglect qualifies as a weapon," Maheu said, "*they killed him*." Hughes was said to have died of kidney failure; however, weighing ninety pounds, with hypodermic needles broken off in his arms, as evident in the autopsy x-rays, sure as hell suggests something else.

I don't think anyone was more touched by the passing of Howard Hughes than Bob Maheu. When he was told of Hughes passing, he broke down and cried. He knew how Hughes had been treated, but he was helpless to do anything about it.

It was comforting for me to have learned that when Bob Maheu died of congestive heart failure on August 6, 2008, in Las Vegas; Hughes aide Gordon Margulis was there at Maheu's bedside when the end came. Gordon Margulis and John Holmes were the only two non-Mormons employed as Hughes aides. Both men were Catholics, as was Maheu.

Nobody has ever been held accountable for the crime of neglect. However, the United States Drug Enforcement Agency (DEA) charged Hughes's physician Dr. Norman Crane and aide John Holmes with providing illegal drugs to Hughes. Both were convicted. Both made a financial settlement with the Hughes estate, and the cases were closed.

Howard Hughes's funeral took place in Houston, Texas. His political friends weren't there. His show business friends weren't there. His Mormon aides weren't there. Only a small number of family members, who he really didn't know, were there. Howard Hughes wanted to be cremated, but his closest relative, Annette Gano Lummis, his mother's sister, insisted he be buried in the family plot. So that's where he is to this day.

As far as the "Mormon Will," or "Melvin Dummar Will," is concerned, which allegedly left one-sixteenth of the Hughes estate to Dumar, the courts found the will to be a forgery, but no court, in any state, has charged Dummar with anything. Two of the expert witness handwriting examiners claim the will is in Hughes's handwriting. However, because the words *Spruce Goose* were used to identify the Hercules H-4 and because Hughes left money to the Boy Scouts of America, an organization he rarely if ever supported, the other two handwriting experts said it was fraudulent.

The Spruce Goose, the Hercules H-4. It never had a splinter of spruce in it. Hughes flew this plane 11/2/47.

Melvin Dummar:
Still Fighting for What
HE FEELS HUGHES
Left Him

I N 2008 DUMMAR APPEALED TO the Ninth Circuit US Court in
Salt Lake City and lost again. He has since appealed to the Tenth
Circuit Court in Denver. The defendants in the case are William
Lummis and Frank Gay, since deceased. Dummar alleges:

A) Fraud

B) Unjust enrichment

C) Racketeering

Dummar requests $156 million, plus interest since 1978, and
punitive damages. Dummar and the Latter Day Saints Church (the
Mormon church) were each to receive $156 million. It is not the
purpose of this book to determine if the "Mormon Will" is authentic.
However, I spoke at length with Melvin, his brother, and nephew,
and, just as the two handwriting experts were convinced the will
was authentic, I am certain Melvin told me the truth; I still believe
it. Hughes had no allegiance to those who were named beneficiaries;

he didn't even know them. Hughes never met any of them, with the exception of Annette Ganno Lumis, his eighty-five-year-old aunt, his mother's sister, now deceased. Hughes hadn't seen his aunt in fifty or more years. Ultimately, William R. Lummis, Annette's son, and a Houston lawyer took over the Hughes-owned Summa Corporation, formerly known as Hughes Nevada Operations, selling off all of the hotels, much of the real estate, and other Hughes holdings in Nevada, Texas, California, and Arizona.

To his credit, Lummis turned the company around; he got rid of the Mormon influence of Bill Gay, Kay Glenn—his Chief Mormons (as Hughes called them), as well as the Hughes aides, two of whom were on the board of directors of the Summa Corporation, until they were replaced by Lummis. Before he retired, William Lummis made millions for the Hughes Corporation.

Who Was
HOWARD ROBARD HUGHES?

HOWARD HUGHES WAS A GREAT American. He was the man the CIA choose to build the super-secret Glomar Explorer, a ship built to raise a Russian submarine from the bottom of the ocean floor, thereby recovering two nuclear torpedoes and cryptographic information for the CIA, as well as the remains of the Russian crew, which were given a military funeral by the United States government.

America will remember Howard Hughes as "The Aviator" because of the movie with Leonardo DiCaprio and from his record-shattering flights, on a par with Charles Lindberg. He'll be remembered as the owner of the RKO Motion Picture Studios on Melrose Avenue in Hollywood. He produced such major pictures as *The Outlaw*," with Jane Russell, *Hell's Angels,* with Jean Harlow, *Front Page,* and *Scarface.* Howard Hughes will be remembered as the builder of the world's biggest airplane, the Hercules HK-1, better known as the

Spruce Goose; however, Hughes hated that name because there wasn't a splinter of spruce in it. This is a hard one to believe, but true—during the filming of *Hell's Angels,* Hughes owned the largest private air force in the world, larger than those of many countries. Hughes will be remembered as the owner of Hughes Tool Company, which revolutionized the oil drilling business. Hughes Aviation was the builder of helicopters for military, police, and television use. Hughes was the owner of TWA and Hughes Air-West. He owned six casinos in Las Vegas (the Desert Inn, the Sands, the Frontier, the Silver Slipper, the Castaways, and the Landmark) and one in Reno (Harold's Club). All are gone now, except for Harold's Club in Reno. It will be noted in history that he founded the Howard Hughes Medical Institute in Houston, Texas, one of the largest philanthropic organizations in the world, with an endowment of $11 billion that spends nearly $500 million annually and saves lives every day. Howard Hughes was the biggest landowner in Nevada, next to the United States government ... and still is today.

To Howard Hughes, the word *impossible* never existed. There were just degrees of difficulty. He had it all: wealth, fame, power, and women. He had everything but someone to really care for him. But even in light of all that, he was a true twentieth-century visionary. Howard Hughes saw the future before it was here ... and there will never be another like him.

THE END

More about John Harris Sheridan and
his books on his web page at:

johnharrissheridan.com

CPSIA information can be obtained
at www.ICGtesting.com
Printed in the USA
LVHW041459090520
655282LV00003B/758